SUPERSTARS
of the NFL

Phil Barber

**Andrews McMeel
Publishing**

Kansas City

NFL Properties Publishing Division
Vice President/Editor-in-Chief: John Wiebusch
General Manager: Bill Barron
Managing Editor: Chuck Garrity, Sr.
Project Editor: Jim Gigliotti

Produced by Lionheart Books, Ltd.
Atlanta, Georgia 30341

Design: Jill Dible

Cover photo: Peter Brouillet

TABLE OF CONTENTS

One Common Denominator and 35 Uncommon Dominators

At first glance, they have no more linking them than 35 random people waiting in line at the Department of Motor Vehicles. Yes, the NFL stars in this book all are outstanding athletes who play the most popular game in America. But they come in more flavors than Jelly Bellies.

They are as compact as Barry Sanders (5 feet 8 inches), as lithe as Merton Hanks (185 pounds), and as gargantuan as Tony Boselli (6-7, 322). They are as young as Eddie George, who turns 25 on September 24, 1998, and as elderly as Warren Moon, who turns 42 less than two months later.

Thirty-five players were selected for this collection, and they have 35 unique stories. Troy Aikman grew up in Henryetta, Oklahoma, which is slightly bigger than Kiln, Mississippi, hometown of Brett Favre. Terrell Davis survived one of San Diego's toughest neighborhoods while Bruce Matthews was enjoying suburban life in Arcadia, California. And then there is Morten Andersen, who grew up in Struer, Denmark, his father a psychologist and his mother a teacher.

Drew Bledsoe was the Walla Walla Wonder, fingered for stardom in high school and later taken with the first pick of the 1993 draft following his career at Washington State. Shannon Sharpe attended Savannah State, a Division II school, and was taken in the seventh round in 1990; he caught a grand total of 29 passes his first two NFL seasons. Moon and John Randle weren't drafted at all. Dan Marino was voted to the Pro Bowl as a rookie. It took Steve Young eight years to get there.

Their personalities are equally diverse. The gregarious Sharpe has yet to find a topic that didn't warrant at least 2,000 words. Contrast him with Barry Sanders, so reserved that he had to be talked into attending the 1988 Heisman Trophy presentation ceremony; naturally, he ended up the guest of honor. Deion Sanders is known for his $5,000 suits and his hit single, "Must Be the Money." Herman Moore is better known for living in a modest apartment and driving a used pickup truck after signing a lucrative rookie contract.

But if you scratch a little deeper, you are bound to find a common thread that binds these men. When the San Diego Chargers traveled to Rocklin, California, to join the San Francisco 49ers for a dual training camp in 1993, learned observers such as John Madden and Bobby Beathard noted a curious phenomenon: The two guys who consistently expended the most effort were Jerry Rice and Junior Seau. In essence, the most talented players also were the hardest workers.

And this is the common denominator you'll find on every page that follows: the drip of sweat. There are a lot of ways to display a Calvinist work ethic. It could be Dorsey Levens enlisting a well-known track coach in an effort to break the Packers' starting lineup. It could be Aeneas Williams phoning experienced defensive backs to pick their brains about technique and strategy. Maybe it's John Randle, dirt-poor child of the East Texas cotton fields, tying a log to his waist and pulling it down the street. Perhaps it's Brett Favre and Reggie White, the guys you would least expect to seek an edge, turning out the lights in the empty Green Bay weight room, as they so often do. Even Deion Sanders is a devoted student of game tapes.

All of this might surprise a lot of people. It's easy to dismiss sports stars as gifted freaks of nature who share nothing with the common folk. Then you learn that what really sets these guys apart isn't size or strength or speed (though you can bet they have those qualities in abundance), but raw effort.

Refreshing, isn't it? The same trait that makes a good farmer or a successful engineer also defines an NFL star.

Troy Aikman

Dallas Cowboys

During his five seasons as head coach of the Dallas Cowboys (1989–93), Jimmy Johnson negotiated 46 trades, drafted 54 college players, signed 29 Plan B free agents, and changed offensive coordinators. It was a major overhaul that would take one of sports' most storied franchises to new lows, quickly followed by incredible highs. But one component was never in doubt: quarterback Troy Aikman.

Aikman was the first player ever drafted by Johnson, and he is at the core of the league's most successful team of this decade.

"The best thing that ever happened to Dallas was getting Troy Aikman," says Roger Staubach, whose Cowboys records Aikman has been busy shattering. "They wouldn't have won one Super Bowl in the nineties without him."

For a while, critics wondered if Aikman could win a game. He missed five games with a broken finger in his rookie season and was 0-11 over the remainder of the schedule. He had moments of glory—he passed for 379 yards against Phoenix—but mostly it was a rotten experience for him and the Cowboys. Only the steadiest of players could have bounced back.

Steady? If some quarterbacks play like movie heroes, Aikman plays like the hero's accountant. He can't throw the ball a mile like Drew Bledsoe. He doesn't have John Elway's flair for last-minute heroics. He doesn't break a lot of tackles in the open field.

"I'm not Steve Young, and I'll never be Steve Young," Aikman says. "In our system the ball comes out right away. I don't sit back and hold it."

In Dallas's system, Aikman's directive is simple: Play smart football and keep the boat on course. That is exactly what he has done.

"Troy doesn't make bad decisions," said Norv Turner in 1993, when he was the Cowboys' offensive coordinator. "All the quarterbacks in this league are capable of making big plays. But Troy has reached a point where he doesn't put us in negative situations."

Aikman knows when to throw away the ball or dump off to a back rather than force a deep pass into coverage. His command of the short, timing routes is absolute. "He's very compact and efficient in his motion," Turner says, "but his biggest strength is accuracy. He's as accurate as any quarterback around, and for a strong-armed guy that's unusual."

> "As a receiver, there is not a quarterback in the league you'd rather have throwing to you."
> — Michael Irvin

Aikman's career completion percentage of 62.01 is the third best in NFL history. His quarterback rating (82.3) ranks tenth on the league's all-time charts. He holds Cowboys records for career attempts (3,696), completions (2,292), yards (26,016), and 3,000-yard seasons (5).

It gets even better in the playoffs. Aikman has been Dallas's Mr. January. In the 1992 postseason, while spurring the Cowboys to victory in Super Bowl XXVII, he completed 61 of 89 passes for 795 yards and 8 touchdowns, with no interceptions. Overall, he has a postseason record of 11-2 as a starter.

"Troy has the whole package," says Michael Irvin, his favorite target. "As a receiver, there is not a quarterback in the league you'd rather have throwing to you."

Aikman was an All-America at UCLA, but his personality is more suited to Henryetta, Oklahoma, the small town where he went to high school. "Troy has a tolerance for bull of somewhere between a second-and-a-half and three seconds," says his agent, Leigh Steinberg.

When it comes to fund raising, the quarterback is much more patient. His Aikman Foundation supports numerous local charities, including the "Aikman End Zone" program, which sets up interactive centers in children's hospitals. His civic efforts brought him the Byron White Humanitarian Award in 1994 and the True Value NFL Man of the Year designation in 1997. The attention is nice, but Aikman remains Aikman.

"The biggest thing about Troy is that he hasn't let superstar status go to his head," Johnson says. "His number-one commitment is to helping the team win. That sets a good example for everybody else."

Yes, Aikman has enjoyed the help of some very talented teammates. But no one questions who is at the heart of Dallas's offense.

"There are few quarterbacks who can bring their teams to play at a higher level with their own performance," Staubach says. "Troy Aikman is one of them. He'll have a lot of records because he's a great passer. But his main asset is his teammates believe he'll win."

They are justified in their belief. Aikman has started in three Super Bowl victories; no other active quarterback has started in more than one. And that, some would say, is the only statistic that matters at football's most important position.

#8 TROY AIKMAN, Quarterback

YEAR	TEAM	ATT	COMP	PCT	YDS	TD	INT	RATING
1989	Dallas	293	155	52.9	1,749	9	18	55.7
1990	Dallas	399	226	56.6	2,579	11	18	66.6
1991	Dallas	363	237	65.3	2,754	11	10	86.7
1992	Dallas	473	302	63.9	3,445	23	14	89.5
1993	Dallas	392	271	69.1	3,100	15	6	99.0
1994	Dallas	361	233	64.5	2,676	13	12	84.9
1995	Dallas	432	280	64.8	3,304	16	7	93.6
1996	Dallas	465	296	63.7	3,126	12	13	80.1
1997	Dallas	518	292	56.4	3,283	19	12	78.0
CAREER TOTALS		3,696	2,292	62.0	26,016	129	110	82.3

Morten Andersen

In 1995, the New Orleans Saints learned that hell hath no fury like a kicker scorned. Hoping to squeeze under the salary cap by forcing him to accept a smaller number, they cut Morten Andersen two days before the start of training camp. But Andersen had no interest in being down-salaried. He contacted the Saints' arch rival, the Atlanta Falcons, and was in a new uniform within 24 hours.

New Orleans fans were shocked. They weren't just losing the leading scorer in club history. They were losing one of their most popular citizens. Andersen had raised more than $400,000 for Children's Hospital through his Kicks for Kids program, and his good looks made him something of a heart throb. A poster of Andersen in a cutoff jersey and shorts sold 16,000 copies, and *New Orleans Magazine* named him one of the city's 10 most eligible bachelors.

Of course, some people were thrilled with the move—namely, the Falcons veterans who had watched Andersen beat their team five times with last-minute kicks. "You can't imagine how depressing it was to watch that guy destroy us game after game," linebacker Jessie Tuggle says.

The Saints soon would know the feeling. In the first of the rivals' two games of 1995, Andersen made 4 of 4 field-goal attempts, the last from 21 yards with 4:02 remaining in overtime to give Atlanta a 27-24 victory. "That was a sweet kick," Andersen said of the game winner. "It really gave me a sense of closure. It helped me exorcise a lot of demons."

The demons were ducking for cover when the teams met again in December. Andersen again was 4 for 4, and this time 3 of them were from beyond 50 yards (55, 55, and 51). It was the first time in NFL history someone had kicked three 50-yard field goals in one game.

As if the Saints had forgotten, Andersen has tremendous leg strength. He is, in fact, an exemplary athlete who was a gymnast and a long jumper in high school in Struer, Denmark, and who narrowly missed making the Danish junior national soccer team.

Andersen never saw an American football until he came to the United States as a 17-year-old exchange student. He was hanging around practice at Ben Davis High School in Indianapolis when the coach spotted him nailing 50-yard kicks, and that was the start of a dream career.

Since joining the Saints as a fourth-round draft choice in 1983, Andersen has established NFL records for scoring in consecutive games (222 and counting), 50-yard field goals in a career (33), 50-yard kicks in a season (5, in 1995), 100-point seasons (11, tied with Nick Lowery), and Pro Bowl appearances by a kicker (7). He has two of the four longest field goals in NFL history, and his kickoffs routinely sail past the goal line.

But it is his 25 game-winning kicks that are most impressive.

"Morten has a different button from most

kickers," says June Jones, former head coach of the Falcons. "More often than not, when the game is on the line, most kickers are pacing, really nervous. Morten is the first kicker I've had who *wants* to kick with the game on the line. What Joe Montana is to quarterbacks, Morten is to kickers."

For Andersen, it isn't so much containing his anxiety as refusing to acknowledge it in the first place. "Doubt will make you unemployed very quickly," he says. "That's why I'm so meticulous about my preparation."

Andersen is a big proponent of visualization. He

walks himself through various kicking scenarios at every practice. All of them end the same way, with the ball traveling end-over-end through the uprights. He is, by all accounts, a cerebral man. He speaks four languages. He was an academic All-America at Michigan State, with a double major in communications and German and a double minor in marketing and French.

Perhaps it is his educational background and rich well of life experiences (he hiked the Himalayas with his father Erik a few years ago) that allow Andersen to put his trade in healthy perspective. "There are one billion Chinese people who couldn't care less about what I do," he likes to say. "My little egocentric endeavors are insignificant. They certainly don't change world events."

Or as his mother Hanne once put it: "It's not really all that important what he does. He kicks a football."

At least Mrs. Andersen can rest assured that her son kicks that ball as well as anyone ever has.

#5 MORTEN ANDERSEN, Kicker

YEAR	TEAM	XPM	XPA	FGM	FGA	LONG	PTS
1982	New Orleans	6	6	2	5	45	12
1983	New Orleans	37	38	18	24	52	91
1984	New Orleans	34	34	20	27	53	94
1985	New Orleans	27	29	31	35	55	120
1986	New Orleans	30	30	26	30	53	108
1987	New Orleans	37	37	28	36	52	121
1988	New Orleans	32	33	26	36	51	110
1989	New Orleans	44	45	20	29	49	104
1990	New Orleans	29	29	21	27	52	92
1991	New Orleans	38	38	25	32	60	113
1992	New Orleans	33	34	29	34	52	120
1993	New Orleans	33	33	28	35	56	117
1994	New Orleans	32	32	28	39	48	116
1995	Atlanta	29	30	31	37	59	122
1996	Atlanta	31	31	22	29	54	97
1997	Atlanta	35	35	23	27	55	104
CAREER TOTALS		507	514	378	482	60	1,641

Jerome Bettis

Pittsburgh Steelers

Dermontti Dawson, the Steelers' Pro Bowl center, remembers a goal-line play at Cincinnati in 1997. It was fourth down from the 1 with Pittsburgh trailing 7-6, and the handoff went to Jerome Bettis. "I just looked up and saw him for a second, and his legs were going a hundred miles per hour," Dawson says. "I knew nothing was going to stop him from getting into the end zone."

Bettis got his six points and the Steelers went on to win 26-10. It wasn't exactly the NFL play of the year, but it was the perfect illustration of the Jerome Bettis style of football. His nickname is "The Bus"—it has been since he played at Notre Dame—and if you value your health you are encouraged to stay out from under his wheels.

"You'd better stop Bettis before he gets started," says Ozzie Newsome, Baltimore's vice president of player personnel. "Once he gets through the line and squares up, he causes some problems. There aren't too many people in the secondary who want to spend their Sunday afternoons tackling Jerome Bettis."

He is 5 feet 11 inches, 245 pounds, with the thighs of a Kodiak bear and the gut of a piano mover. Bettis has surprisingly nimble moves, too, but the basis of his game is the straight-ahead rumble.

"After you tackle him you're laughing and joking with him," veteran NFL safety Eugene Robinson says. "But on your way to the huddle you're thinking, 'Oh, boy, I'm in trouble.'"

Bettis was an NFL star from the outset. He rushed for 1,429 yards as a rookie in 1993 and 1,025 yards in his second season, both with the

Rams. But he fell out of favor with the Rams and his carries declined.

The usually jovial runner was at an emotional low, but he was recharged by a trade to Pittsburgh in 1996. Steelers director of football operations Tom Donahoe heard nothing but praise about Bettis. "He's a real friendly kid," says Joe Moore, the former Notre Dame assistant who recruited Bettis. "He's easygoing off the field, easy to get along with, and has a nice personality."

So for the price of second- and fourth-round picks, the Steelers got a workhorse ball carrier. And Bettis, only 24 at the time, got a new lease on life.

"After you tackle him you're laughing and joking with him," veteran NFL safety Eugene Robinson says. "But on your way to the huddle you're thinking, 'Oh, boy, I'm in trouble.'"

"We had to have him," Pittsburgh head coach Bill Cowher says. "You win championships with people, and they don't come any finer than Jerome."

Bettis has flourished in the Steelers' game plan. He finished second to Denver's Terrell Davis among AFC rushers each of the last two seasons, with 1,431 yards in 1996 and 1,665 in 1997. The latter figure was a mere 25 yards shy of Barry Foster's club record, and Bettis sat out one game. He also has scored 20 touchdowns in two seasons.

"His style is made to order for what they want to do," Indianapolis defensive tackle Tony McCoy says. "He is going to pound

on you. He makes them a tough team to beat."

For his part, Bettis extends the comfort zone from the offense to the entire city. "I'm a blue-collar player, and this is a blue-collar town," he says.

How blue-collar is Bettis? His second-favorite game is bowling. When he was a kid, his mother Gladys took him to Detroit's Central City Lanes, mainly to keep him off the streets. Bettis grew to love the alleys. He averages about 200, and in 1995 he rolled a perfect 300 during a pro-am event in Michigan.

Meanwhile, Steelers' fans have gleefully adopted Bettis. They buy Bus caps and T-shirts like they once snapped up Terrible Towels. When St. Louis came to town in 1996, someone hung a banner at Three Rivers Stadium that read: "Blitzburg Thanks the Rams for the Gift That Keeps on Giving 100 Yards a Game: No. 36."

Bettis responded with 129 yards in a 42-6 victory.

To show appreciation for his full-throttle career,

Bettis has lavished gifts upon his offensive linemen and Tim Lester, the fullback who has blocked for him with both the Rams and the Steelers. He has bought them big-screen televisions, expensive dinners, and trips to Honolulu for the Pro Bowl. At least one of those linemen, however, doesn't see what all the fuss is about.

"As hard as he runs," guard Will Wolford says, "he's his own blocker."

#36 JEROME BETTIS, Running Back

| YEAR | TEAM | RUSHING | | | | RECEIVING | | | |
		NO	YDS	AVG	TD	NO	YDS	AVG	TD
1993	L.A. Rams	294	1,429	4.9	7	26	244	9.4	0
1994	L.A. Rams	319	1,025	3.2	3	31	293	9.5	1
1995	St. Louis	183	637	3.5	3	18	106	5.9	0
1996	Pittsburgh	320	1,431	4.5	11	22	122	5.5	0
1997	Pittsburgh	375	1,665	4.4	7	15	110	7.3	2
CAREER TOTALS		1,491	6,187	4.1	31	112	875	7.8	3

Drew Bledsoe

New England Patriots

If you had to pinpoint the date when Patriots quarterback Drew Bledsoe "arrived," it would be November 13, 1994. On that day the Patriots, already staggering at 3-6, fell behind Minnesota 20-0. Coach Bill Parcells had seen enough. With less than a minute left in the first half, he ordered a hurry-up offense — and Bledsoe went wild. In the latter stages of the game he passed on 34 consecutive plays. He completed his first 6 passes in overtime and hit Kevin Turner for the winning touchdown at 4:10 of the extra period.

Bledsoe finished the game with NFL records for attempts (70) and completions (45). By the end of 1994, he had set a league mark with 691 attempts in a season. He has been one of the sport's most productive quarterbacks ever since.

Anything less, of course, would be considered a failure for Bledsoe, who was fitted for a superstar's cleats years ago. His football background started early: at age 3 he attended a football camp led by his father, Mac (who would later become his high school coach). In the seventh grade, Drew was beaten out for the starting quarterback position; it never would happen again.

By the time Bledsoe got to Washington State he was the Walla Walla Wonder, a strapping phenom who was destined for the NFL. And when he became the first pick in the 1993 draft, he brought a ton of expectations with him.

Bob Ryan, a *Boston Globe* columnist, welcomed

Bledsoe by writing, "Only injury will prevent Drew Bledsoe from becoming the Patriots' answer to Teddy, Bobby, and Larry."

Ryan was referring to the Boston Holy Trinity of baseball's Ted Williams, hockey's Bobby Orr, and basketball's Larry Bird. When Bledsoe heard the prediction, he rolled his eyes and said, "I wish people would wait until I do something before making these comparisons."

He's done a few things since then, such as taking his team to the playoffs three times in five seasons, when it hadn't been to postseason play in the six years prior to his arrival. Twice he has thrown for more than 4,000 yards (in 1994 and 1996). After the '94 season he became the youngest quarterback ever to play in the Pro Bowl. (Dan Marino was 7 months younger when he was voted to his first Pro Bowl, but a knee injury kept him out of the game.) During a seven-game span in 1995, Bledsoe set a club record by throwing 179 consecutive passes without an interception.

"He can throw any kind of pass," former Patriots quarterback Steve Grogan says.

> "He can throw any kind of pass. Drew reminds me of a young Marino. He has a knack of seeing the field and delivering the ball."
> — Steve Grogan

"Drew reminds me of a young Marino. He has a knack of seeing the field and delivering the ball. He also seems to have a real good head on his shoulders. He hasn't let his successes affect him or his failures drag him down."

Physically dragging him down is a difficult problem. He is 6 feet 5 inches, 233 pounds, and rugged enough to have started the Patriots' last 44 games (the longest streak among AFC quarterbacks). But Bledsoe has persistent detractors. They say that he forces the ball into coverage and that he throws too many interceptions. More significantly, they claim he tends to self-destruct in critical games. The facts say otherwise.

Bledsoe and the Patriots lost to Green Bay in Super Bowl XXXI, but could anyone have beaten the Packers that day? Anyway, at 24 he was the third-youngest quarterback to start in a Super Bowl. What's more, Bledsoe has a career record of 14-6 in December, the NFL's make-or-break month. He's superb in the two-minute drill, and last season he led the AFC in completion percentage (60.2), yards (1,242), and touchdowns (10) on third-down plays. That's performance under pressure.

"He's one of the few people I know on earth who has an inner calm," says Bledsoe's agent, Leigh Steinberg.

That serene posture helps Bledsoe, the prototype quarterback of the nineties, keep his life and work in perspective.

"Win or lose," Bledsoe says, "when I come home my dogs will jump all over me."

#11 DREW BLEDSOE, Quarterback

YEAR	TEAM	ATT	COMP	PCT	YDS	TD	INT	RATING
1993	New England	429	214	49.9	2,494	15	15	65.0
1994	New England	691	400	57.9	4,555	25	27	73.6
1995	New England	636	323	50.8	3,507	13	16	63.7
1996	New England	623	373	59.9	4,086	27	15	83.7
1997	New England	522	314	60.2	3,706	28	15	87.7
CAREER TOTALS		2,901	1,624	56.0	18,348	108	88	74.9

Tony Boselli

Jacksonville Jaguars

A ngi Aylor had been dating Tony Boselli for about four months, and she knew he was a football player. She just didn't know if he was any good. He told her he was a "fringe player." Then Aylor went to a Fourth of July party and met a couple of players from Stanford. "My boyfriend plays for USC," she told them, "but you probably haven't heard of him. His name is Tony Boselli."

The Cardinal players' jaws dropped. They directed Aylor to the nearest newsstand, where she picked up a copy of a college football preview magazine. Her boyfriend was on the cover. Inside, the magazine said he might be the best player in the conference.

Aylor later became Miss California 1994, and after that Mrs. Tony Boselli. And she still can't believe the way she was duped. Only an offensive tackle could have pulled it off.

But Boselli is so good, so unique, that even the trenches no longer can hide him. At 26 he might be the best offensive lineman in the NFL.

"He is the guy who I've seen come out recently who will be around a long, long time," legendary tackle Anthony Muñoz says. "It's all technique. You can be big, strong, and athletic, but if you have poor technique you can't block anybody. Tony has it. I've watched him. He's great already, and he'll only get better."

Muñoz, of course, preceded Boselli at USC. So did offensive linemen such

as Bruce Matthews, Roy Foster, and Don Mosebar. And yet John Robinson, who coached all of them, described Boselli as "the best college lineman I've ever had."

At 6 feet 7 inches, 326 pounds, his appeal was obvious to NFL scouts. But when Jaguars head coach Tom Coughlin met with Boselli and watched him work out, it wasn't the massive frame

that left him shaking his head. "The key for me was the maturity he had that was beyond his years — the poise, the attitude," the coach says. "Tony brought a lot to the table."

So Coughlin and the Jaguars took Boselli with the second pick in 1995, making him the highest-drafted offensive lineman since Tony Mandarich in 1989. More significantly, Boselli became the inaugural draft choice in the history of the Jacksonville franchise. "He's the cornerstone," Coughlin said as the team signed him to the richest contract ever for a rookie offensive lineman: $17 million over seven years.

It was money well spent. At left tackle, Boselli routinely faces the NFL's most devastating pass rushers—and he routinely leaves them frustrated and fruitless. This never was more evident than in the 1996 playoffs, when the Jaguars took to the road to play the Bills and Broncos. In those two games Boselli went up against Bruce Smith and Alfred Williams, who had combined for 26½ sacks in the regular season. (Smith was consensus NFL defensive player of the year.) Neither of them laid a hand on Mark Brunell, and Jacksonville emerged with consecutive upset victories.

"Tony is a very, very large human being," Coughlin says, "but he moves with the grace of someone smaller. Here's a man fifty pounds heavier than any premier NFL pass rusher, but he has the athleticism, maneuverability, and speed to compete with them."

Boselli always has been known as a technically superb pass blocker. It was his run blocking that some questioned, and so that is where he worked—and worked, and worked. He practiced his leverage and his footwork. He lowered his stance and rehearsed his steps until he was a force on the run, too.

Where did Boselli get such a work ethic? Maybe it was the two summers he spent gardening, baling hay, and rounding up calves for the Benedictine nuns of the Abbey of St. Walburga, just outside Boulder, Colorado. "There were days at the con-

"Tony is a very, very large human being," Coughlin says, "but he moves with the grace of someone smaller."

vent when the nuns worked me harder than the USC coaching staff did," Boselli says.

More likely, it has to do with his churning desire to be the best. "He's a Pro Bowl player," Jacksonville guard Ben Coleman says, "but you still see him after practice, working on different techniques, studying the opponent because he wants to be able to take care of his business."

Boselli knows there is little that separates the good NFL players from the great ones these days. "The position I play is all about consistency," says the man who recently went more than 36 games without missing an offensive play. "The only thing people remember is your last game and your last year.

"That's all I concern myself with: How am I going to play in the next game?"

Tim Brown

Oakland Raiders

Jeff Hostetler was a hard-nosed overachiever who excelled at throwing on the run. Jeff George is a classic dropback passer with a strong arm and a mercurial temperament. The two quarterbacks couldn't have more disparate styles, but they have one thing in common (beyond their first name): They both name Tim Brown as the best receiver with whom they've played.

"He has size, speed, the ability to run with the ball, and a sense of where to find open holes," Hostetler says as evidence.

"He can do it all," George says. "He can play outside, he can play slot. You can put him in the backfield and run routes that way. He's got what it takes."

Brown has played catch with a lot of quarterbacks during his tenure in Oakland—Jay Schroeder, Todd Marinovich, Vince Evans are a few more examples—and all of them would likely rank him at the top. They simply don't come much better equipped than number 81.

Some players are game-breakers, others are reliable possession receivers. Brown is one of the few who can fill both roles. He is a dangerous runner after the catch, too. And this is after a 1989 knee injury that, he claims, permanently impaired his speed.

Before that setback, everything had come easy for the kid who once dreamed of being "Twinkletoes Brown," star Cowboys running back. He was an All-America runner for Woodrow Wilson High School in Dallas, and he spent four storied years at Notre Dame. He won the 1987

Heisman Trophy and departed with school records for receiving yards (2,493), kickoff-return yards (1,613), and all-purpose yards (5,024).

The Raiders made Brown the first wide receiver taken in a rich 1988 draft that included the likes of Sterling Sharpe, Michael Irvin, and Anthony Miller, and he made the NFL seem like nothing more than a giant playground. Brown finished the year as the NFL leader in kick-off returns (a 26.8-yard average), the AFC leader in punt-return yardage (444), and the Raiders' leader in receptions (43). His 2,317 all-purpose yards broke the

"He'll freeze a guy like he's in slow motion," former Raiders linebacker Rob Fredrickson says. "Then he has a sudden burst of speed. He's great at changing speeds and changing directions."

league rookie record formerly held by Hall of Famer Gale Sayers.

But in the first game of 1989 Brown tore his posterior cruciate and medial collateral ligaments. He missed the rest of the season and didn't start the next two as he regained his strength.

Now that seems like ancient history. Brown has led the AFC in receiving yardage in four of the last five seasons. He had his best year ever in 1997, when George found him 104 times for 1,408 yards. Both figures were club records, and the reception total tied him (with Herman Moore) for the NFL lead.

You would expect opponents to double-team Brown—and they do. That constantly opens up routes for tight end Rickey Dudley and fellow wide receiver James Jett, but it doesn't necessarily ensure that Brown will be shut down.

"He's one of the only receivers I know who can get open against double coverage," Jets cornerback Aaron Glenn says. "He can make moves and get open. I don't know how he does it, but he does."

Some defenses will even send a linebacker out wide to hamper Brown at the line. The Raiders counter by frequently sending him in motion, but often it is Brown's resourcefulness that gets him free. His signature "double move"—fake inside, fake back outside, cut upfield—has been known to leave defensive backs twisted into abstract art pieces.

"He'll freeze a guy like he's in slow motion," former Raiders linebacker Rob Fredrickson says. "Then he has a sudden burst of speed. He's great at changing speeds and changing directions."

At least opposing special teams don't have to worry about him anymore. Brown was a two-time Pro Bowl choice as a kick returner, but he relinquished kickoff returns long ago, and he handed over punt returns to Desmond Howard last season. Before passing the torch, however, Brown returned more punts (301) than any other man in NFL history. He still is the only Raiders player ever to score on a reception, a handoff, a punt return, and a kickoff return.

Yes, Twinkletoes Brown has won just about every honor imaginable for a football player. But the big one has eluded him. He never has won a championship, not at any level. It is a pursuit that consumes him, and if he has to carry the Raiders there on his back, that's fine with him.

"I like being the go-to guy," Brown says. "It puts pressure on me, but that's why you play this game."

#81 TIM BROWN, Wide Receiver

YEAR	TEAM	NO	YDS	AVG	TD
1988	L.A. Raiders	43	725	16.9	5
1989	L.A. Raiders	1	8	8.0	0
1990	L.A. Raiders	18	265	14.7	3
1991	L.A. Raiders	36	554	15.4	5
1992	L.A. Raiders	49	693	14.1	7
1993	L.A. Raiders	80	1,180	14.8	7
1994	L.A. Raiders	89	1,309	14.7	9
1995	Oakland	89	1,342	15.1	10
1996	Oakland	90	1,104	12.3	9
1997	Oakland	104	1,408	13.5	5
CAREER TOTALS		599	8,588	14.3	60

Mark Brunell

Jacksonville Jaguars

During the 1996 season, a television analyst asked Jacksonville quarterback Mark Brunell how it felt to have one of the NFL's best left tackles, Tony Boselli, protecting his blindside. One problem: Brunell is a left-handed passer. Boselli protects his frontside.

The analyst can be forgiven for his oversight, for at that point Brunell still was relatively unknown, even as he authored a season that would make him the first man since Johnny Unitas in 1962 to lead all NFL quarterbacks in both passing yards (4,367) and rushing yards (396). The anonymity wouldn't last much longer, however.

In the first round of the AFC playoffs, Brunell led the Jaguars to victory over the Bills in Rich Stadium, where no visiting team ever had won a postseason game. In the second round, he sparked a 30-27 upset of the mighty Broncos, an outcome some called pro football's biggest postseason upset since Super Bowl III.

"We never faced a quarterback like that before," Denver defensive end Alfred Williams said after the game.

They also never wanted to see another. Brunell repeatedly squirmed away from pass rushers that day. He zipped downfield for big first downs and launched dead-on passes into the end zone, showing a national televi-

sion audience what the Jaguars fans had been seeing for more than a year. A month later he increased the exposure by earning most-valuable-player honors in the Pro Bowl.

Brunell had been such a secret because, before

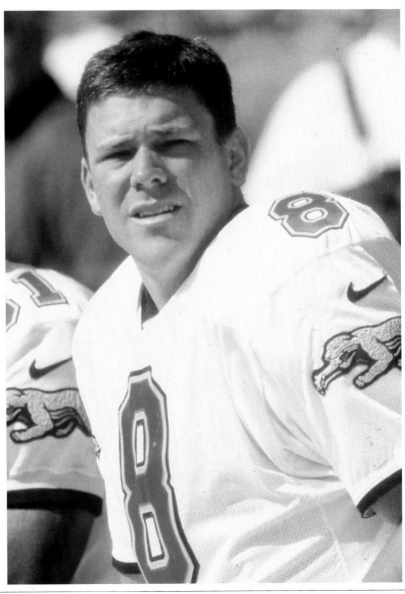

coming to Jacksonville in April, 1995, circumstances had conspired to keep him in the background. He led the Washington Huskies to a Rose Bowl victory as a college sophomore, but he injured his knee during the following spring practice and wound up splitting time with Billy Joe Hobert.

When the Green Bay Packers drafted Brunell in the third round in 1993, he found himself playing second fiddle to the maestro, Brett Favre. Brunell

never started in two seasons. He passed for only 95 yards.

But some NFL people never let him fall off the radar screen. One of them was Jaguars head coach Tom Coughlin, who was busy building a franchise from scratch. "I had spent much of the past year trying to find a quarterback who would be a leader in all ways," Coughlin says. "Without question, of the players who might be available, he was the guy

I wanted as the quarterback of the future here."

The Jaguars got Brunell for the paltry price of a third- and a fifth-round draft choice. It was the first trade ever made by Jacksonville, and it may go down as its best. In the fifth week of the Jaguars' first season, Brunell led the franchise to its first victory—17-16 over the Oilers—and a year later he carried it to the AFC Championship Game.

Brunell has been compared to Steve Young, except he isn't wasting much of his youth waiting for a Joe Montana to retire. Brunell is a fearless leader, a good touch passer, and a sensational scrambler who has been clocked at 4.58 seconds in the 40-yard dash. "When he is running free, it frightens you to death," Redskins cornerback Cris Dishman says.

"Sometimes I have to stop to watch him," Jacksonville wide receiver Jimmy Smith says.

Off the field, however, the loose cannon becomes a strict adherent of Christian canons. Brunell leads 15 to 20 Jaguars teammates in regular Bible study. He had a 3.92 grade-point average in high school. He is a devoted family man who worked construction and roofing jobs as a college senior to support his wife and child.

Brunell needed all of his inner strength in 1997. He suffered a severe knee injury in August, and after he returned (ahead of schedule, thanks to four hours a day of rehabilitative work) he suffered a severely bruised buttock and a dislocated middle finger on his passing hand. When he played, the tender knee took away much of the mobility that had made him so dangerous.

Instead of despairing, Brunell focused on becoming a better dropback passer. He finished the season first in the AFC with a passer rating of 91.2, throwing 18 touchdown passes against 7 interceptions.

"He has his faith and his family and football, and that is all he needs," Jaguars senior vice president Michael Huyghue says. "Some people need training wheels on their bike before thay can ride. Mark just got right on his bike and started doing tricks."

> "When he is running free, it frightens you to death," Redskins cornerback Cris Dishman says. "Sometimes I have to stop to watch him," Jacksonville wide receiver Jimmy Smith says.

#8 MARK BRUNELL, Quarterback

YEAR	TEAM	ATT	COMP	PCT	YDS	TD	INT	RATING
1993	Green Bay — Did not play							
1994	Green Bay	27	12	44.4	95	0	0	53.8
1995	Jacksonville	346	201	58.1	2,168	15	7	82.6
1996	Jacksonville	557	353	63.4	4,367	19	20	84.0
1997	Jacksonville	435	264	60.7	3,281	18	7	91.2
CAREER TOTALS		1,365	830	60.1	9,911	52	34	85.3

Cris Carter 80

It wasn't as cheap as the phone call that supposedly brought Hall of Fame quarterback Johnny Unitas to Baltimore in 1956, but the $100 the Vikings spent to acquire Cris Carter in 1990 has to be rated one of the great sports deals of the century.

Carter, who had played three seasons in Philadelphia, suddenly found himself on the waiver wire the week before the start of the 1990 season.

Stunned by being waived, Carter rededicated himself to the game. Known for less-than-heroic efforts on the practice field, he vowed to work harder. He stopped eating red meat. He gave up alcohol. He cut down on sweets and began a determined fitness regimen.

Carter displayed the same dedication off the field. By 1995, he was accepting the Bart Starr Award from Athletes in Action for outstanding leadership and character on and off the field. He was ordained a minister in 1996. He has committed much of his time to local charities (largely through the Carter-White Charitable Foundation, which he founded with safety William White), and he has become the Vikings' unquestioned locker-room leader.

"I thank him for my success," says teammate Jake Reed, another productive receiver. "He makes me sit down and think about my life. One thing about Cris: He's not going to tell you what you *want* to hear; he'll tell you what you *need* to hear."

Happily, Carter's career has blossomed along with his improved attitude. At the beginning of the 1994 season he was considered a good receiver. By the end of the year he was hailed as one of the game's big-time performers. Carter set an NFL record (since broken) with 122 catches in 1994, and has followed it with totals of 122 (again), 96, and 89. He owns Vikings records for career recep-

tions (667), yards (7,986), and touchdown catches (70).

"Cris is like the small forward in basketball," Vikings head coach Dennis Green says. "He always wants the ball: 'Get it to me down low. Get it to me coming off the post. Get it to me in the lane. Get it to me on an Alley-Oop. Just get it to me because if you get it to me I'll

make the play.' That's his approach to the game."

The basketball analogy is an appropriate one, since Carter's oldest brother Butch starred under Bobby Knight at Indiana and played seven seasons in the NBA.

Cris showed some court moves himself when he won the 1995 Foot Locker Slam Dunk Competition. It

is that leaping ability, along with his size (6 feet 3 inches, 208 pounds), that make Carter the most dangerous goal-line receiver in the game. He led the NFL in touchdown receptions two of the last three seasons, with 17 in 1995 and 13 in 1997. Last year he added three 2-point conversions.

"You never want to cover him inside your twenty-yard line because he has such great leaping ability," new Raiders cornerback Eric Allen says. "The only thing you can do is play the ball and hope you can get it before he does."

And even when the opponent appears to have position, Carter often finds a way to make the catch. "Cris is very acrobatic," says Jerry Rhome, his former receivers coach. "It doesn't seem to bother him to have defenders around. He can jump through the roof, and he has stretching ability. He can make his arms long and his hands long."

Expandable digits? Hey, anything seems possi-ble for a man who has risen from the NFL scrap heap, stretching his life and career to their full potential.

#80 CRIS CARTER, Wide Receiver

YEAR	TEAM	NO	YDS	AVG	TD
1987	Philadelphia	5	84	16.8	2
1988	Philadelphia	39	761	19.5	6
1989	Philadelphia	45	605	13.4	11
1990	Minnesota	27	413	15.3	3
1991	Minnesota	72	962	13.4	5
1992	Minnesota	53	681	12.9	6
1993	Minnesota	86	1,071	12.5	9
1994	Minnesota	122	1,256	10.3	7
1995	Minnesota	122	1,371	11.2	17
1996	Minnesota	96	1,163	12.1	10
1997	Minnesota	89	1,069	12.0	13
CAREER TOTALS		756	9,436	12.5	89

Ben Coates

In 1991, the Patriots' brain trust got word of a tight end prospect in Salisbury, North Carolina. The player was big, fast, and generally athletic, the scouts reported. But he still was considered a gamble because of his lack of experience. He hadn't played football until his senior year of high school. He put aside his pads during his junior year of college to concentrate on basketball and track. And he faced practically no credible competition at Division II Livingstone College.

"Dante [Scarnecchia] was coaching tight ends at the time, and we sent him down there," says Joe Mendes, New England's personnel director in '91. "We told him, 'You don't have to work him out. You don't have to watch any film. Just spend a day with him and find out, can you coach him?'

"So Dante works him out, and then he's even more in love with him. He comes back and says, 'No question, this guy can play for me.'"

As it turns out, the young tight end—Ben Coates—could play for anybody in the universe.

"He's a nightmare to cover," says Todd Collins, the Patriots' linebacker who has to take on Coates at practice. "He's so big that he can push you off him, and he can catch everything high. [Coates is 6 feet 5 inches, 245 pounds.] You can try to use two people, three people on him, but Drew [Bledsoe] throws to him anyway because Ben is like a vacuum cleaner when the ball comes his way. No matter who's doing what, he sucks it in."

New England cornerback Jimmy Hitchcock is

more succinct in his assessment: "He's the best player I've ever seen."

Coates, a fifth-round draft choice in 1991, had little impact during his first two years in the league. But his development was helped by the arrival of two men, Bill Parcells and Drew Bledsoe, in 1993. Parcells, the new head coach, had a history of relying on big tight ends. Bledsoe, then a rookie quarterback, opened up the field with his cannon-strong arm. Parcells gave Coates a chance; Bledsoe helped make him a star.

Coates led the Patriots with 53 receptions in '93, but it was the next season that sent him into a higher orbit. He was sensational in 1994, catching 96 passes (most ever for a tight end), good for 1,174 yards and 7 touchdowns. Suddenly, the secret was out.

"I don't know where that guy came from," Bills

running back Thurman Thomas said after a game that year, "but you can send him to Hawaii right now."

Actually, Coates had to wait until February to play in the Pro Bowl, but he's been back every year since. He leads all NFL tight ends with 308 catches and 30 touchdowns over the last four seasons, and he currently ranks second on the Patriots' career receptions list with 391. He already holds club records for most catches in a season (96), most in a game (12, at Indianapolis in 1994), and most consecutive games with a reception (63).

"Any quarterback in the league would love to throw to the guy," Bledsoe says. "He's always going

to catch the ball, and then one out of every two passes he's going to break two or three tackles and make a big play."

Coates is not one of these wide-receivers-by-another-name who flourish in the West Coast offense. He also can be a devastating block-er—which makes it all the more shocking the first time you get a good look at his speed.

"Like in practice," Hitchcock says, "I'm watching him get by me, and then the ball is thrown and I'm thinking, 'There's no way he's going to get that because it's going to be way over his head.' And then you see him extend that body and he catches it. It's an amazing thing."

Thus the basic dilemma that Coates presents to an opposing defense: Cover him with a big line-backer and he'll leave the guy in the dust; put a small, speedy safety on him and Coates will knock him aside like an inflatable doll.

"He's a tight end who's like an extra offensive lineman, and a tight end who's like an extra wide receiver," Bledsoe says.

The Patriots seemed to be taking Coates's ver-satility a step further when they lined him up at fullback to open a game last September. He was only a decoy on the play, but it got some people wondering what would happen if they gave the big guy a handoff.

"I guarantee you there would be no negative yardage," one teammate says, "and a lot of defen-sive linemen would be hurting after the play."

#87 BEN COATES, Tight End

YEAR	TEAM	NO	YDS	AVG	TD
1991	New England	10	95	9.5	1
1992	New England	20	171	8.6	3
1993	New England	53	659	12.4	8
1994	New England	96	1,174	12.2	7
1995	New England	84	915	10.9	6
1996	New England	62	682	11.0	9
1997	New England	66	737	11.2	8
CAREER TOTALS		391	4,433	11.3	42

Terrell Davis

Denver Broncos

It may go down as the most famous migraine headache in history. It happened to Terrell Davis before tens of millions of television viewers, and it very nearly changed the outcome of Super Bowl XXXII.

The Broncos were marching toward a go-ahead touchdown early in the game when Davis was sandwiched between Green Bay defenders Santana Dotson and LeRoy Butler after setting up first-and-goal at the Packers' 5-yard line. Davis had suffered from migraines since childhood, and he felt the familiar pain, observed the dreaded breakup of his visual field. And while he rested on the bench, then in the locker room, it was hugely apparent that Denver was a different team in his absence.

With Davis, the Broncos built a 14-7 lead; without him, they stalled, failing to gain a single first down and watching the Packers climb to within 17-14; with him again in the second half, they pulled out a memorable 31-24 victory. Davis's output—30 carries for 157 yards and a Super Bowl–record 3 rushing touchdowns—established him as the game's most valuable player.

The Packers had only themselves to blame. In 1995, as the NFL draft moved through the fifth round, Green Bay director of college scouting John Dorsey had suggested Davis, then a senior from Georgia. But he was overruled by general manager Ron Wolf. The Packers opted for The Citadel's Travis Jervey, leaving Davis to fall to the Broncos in the sixth round.

"I'd like to say it was great scouting," says Bob Ferguson, Denver's personnel director when Davis was drafted, "but if we'd known he'd turn out like he has, we would've picked him earlier. We weren't exactly geniuses."

In all, 19 running backs were drafted ahead of Davis that year. It seems absurd now that runners such as Ryan Christopherson, Corey Schlesinger, and Dino Philyaw would be drafted ahead of a future Super Bowl MVP, but nothing in

"You can't really arm-tackle him," Steelers linebacker Levon Kirkland says. "You have to kind of run through him."

Davis's background gave him the look of greatness.

He didn't play football until his junior year of high school; then he played six positions, including nose tackle. Davis went to Long Beach State to play for the one man who believed in him, George Allen. But Allen died a few months later, and Long Beach dropped its football program the next year. Davis transferred to Georgia but was hidden, first behind halfback Garrison Hearst, then behind the passing

of Eric Zeier. And when he did get chances, they often were cut short by injuries. He gained only 445 yards his senior year.

So it wasn't until his first NFL season that the world was able to appreciate what Terrell Davis brings to the game. You have to start with his strength. Though he is 5 feet 11 inches, 200 pounds, Davis runs like a much bigger man.

"When I am out there, I think I have a nose guard's or lineman's mentality," he says.

"You can't really arm-tackle him," Steelers linebacker Levon Kirkland says. "You have to kind of run through him."

And that's easier said than done because Davis has exceptional vision and cutting ability. Denver's rushing scheme is premised upon herding the defensive linemen outside, then having the runner cut upfield against the flow. Nobody does that better than Davis.

"He has great vision," Pittsburgh head coach Bill

Cowher says. "It just takes one guy not to get across the face of a block or one guy to be out of position, and he can hit a hole very quickly."

The quiet, self-effacing runner has proved to be such a perfect fit in Mike Shanahan's offense that his numbers are escalating at an astonishing rate. Davis went from 1,117 yards in 1995 to 1,538 in 1996 to 1,750 in 1997, setting club records the last two years. He flirted with the 2,000-yard plateau last year before separating his shoulder in a week-15 loss to San Francisco. He reached 4,000 yards in 41 games; only Eric Dickerson (33), Jim Brown (38), and Walter Payton (39) got there faster. He became the first Broncos rusher to post a 200-yard game when he pierced the Bengals for 215 yards on September 21, 1997; five weeks later he racked up 207 yards against the Bills. He also tied for the NFL lead with 15 rushing touchdowns in 1997.

"It's funny to me," Davis says of his NFL fortunes. "Sometimes I'm sitting at home, and I'll just laugh. If I'm dreaming, don't wake me up."

"He's the best back in football as far as I'm concerned, bar none," Denver quarterback John Elway says. "He makes us such a balanced team."

About the only major feat still eluding the Broncos' back is an NFL rushing title. Detroit's Barry Sanders narrowly edged him in 1996, gaining 175 yards in the final Monday night game to take the honor by 15 yards.

Think Davis is fretting?

"I couldn't care less about the rushing title," he says calmly. "I am not here to win rushing titles. I am here to help the team win games."

"There's not an ounce of selfishness in him," Shanahan says.

When Davis helped Denver win the biggest game of all, he did it about 15 minutes away from where he grew up in the gritty San Diego neighborhood of Lincoln Heights, which one police spokesman described as the poorest in the city. He originally had attended Morse High School, but saw himself turning into a delinquent.

"I even flunked PE," Davis says. "That's how bad it was."

So he transferred to Lincoln High, a small school best known as the training ground of Marcus Allen. A decade later Davis returned to Lincoln to have his old jersey (number 7) retired in a public ceremony. And five days after that he became the first Super Bowl MVP to win the award in his hometown.

"It's funny to me," Davis says of his NFL fortunes. "Sometimes I'm sitting at home, and I'll just laugh. If I'm dreaming, don't wake me up."

#30 TERRELL DAVIS, Running Back

YEAR	TEAM	RUSHING				RECEIVING			
		NO	YDS	AVG	TD	NO	YDS	AVG	TD
1995	Denver	237	1,117	4.7	7	49	367	7.5	1
1996	Denver	345	1,538	4.5	13	36	310	8.6	2
1997	Denver	369	1,750	4.7	15	42	287	6.8	0
CAREER TOTALS		951	4,405	4.6	35	127	964	7.6	3

Dermontti Dawson

Pittsburgh Steelers

We all know about NFL linemen. They snarl. They curse. They take candy from babies. Unless they are Steelers center Dermontti Dawson—in which case they bake cookies in their spare time and make plans to open a greeting card shop.

"He always has a smile on his face," Pittsburgh offensive line coach Kent Stephenson says. "He's one of those guys you know won't have an ulcer when he gets older. His attitude rubs off on all of us."

Dawson is so pleasant that his nickname in the Steelers' locker room is Ned Flanders, after the irrepressibly affable Simpsons character who is usually heard gushing, "Howdy, neighbor!"

"I have a big problem with players who talk, talk, and talk or push you around at the end of the play," says Dawson, who claims to have inherited his cheery nature from his Grandma Pauline. "I like players who concentrate on their own efforts."

Of course, when you're one of the best players in the NFL, you don't need to talk. "You can argue that a couple centers may be as good as Dermontti, but nobody is better," Steelers guard Will Wolford says of his six-time Pro Bowl teammate. "That is a given."

When Dawson was playing guard at the University of Kentucky, his coach, Jerry Claiborne, used him as a one-man training film, running the projector and telling his other linemen, "This is how it's done."

At Pittsburgh, Dawson's speed allows the team

to run sweeps that most teams only can dream about. And at 6 feet 2 inches and 288 pounds, he more than holds his own in pass blocking.

"Sometimes I sit back and think, 'This guy is going to be in the Hall of Fame, and here I am next to him,'" Steelers guard Brendan Stai says. "It's a great honor."

The Pittsburgh fans might be less overwhelmed, but they have been spoiled by their snappers. Since 1964, the Steelers have had only three starting centers: Ray Mansfield, Mike Webster, and Dawson, who claimed the starting job in 1989. Mansfield played in a franchise-record 182 consecutive games; Webster is in the Hall of Fame. Dawson is more than worthy as a successor.

"Dermontti is a much better athlete than either Raymond or Mike," says former Steelers head coach Chuck Noll, who worked with all three. "Raymond was a heady player. He'd find a way to get the job done. Mike had great strength and power. Dermontti has it all—smarts, strength, quickness, and speed."

"I've never coached a center like him," adds Stephenson, who is in his thirty-fourth season of coaching. "He has outstanding quickness, which is a real key for the center position. He has unbelievable power and explosion.

"Dermontti is not a classic three-hundred-pound offensive lineman. There are people who are 'country strong' and people who are 'weight-room strong.' Dermontti is country strong."

Dawson grew up in Lexington, Kentucky, where he became a high school All-America in the shot put and discus. His family—including wife Regina and two children—lives in Lexington in the offseason, preferring the quiet, unglamorous life just as Dermontti prefers the anonymity of the offensive line.

Dawson's idea of success is to strap on a helmet and do his job every Sunday—and few are better at

> "Dermontti is not a classic three-hundred-pound offensive lineman. There are people who are 'country strong' and people who are 'weight-room strong.' Dermontti is country strong."
> — Chuck Noll

it. Over the last 10 seasons, he has started 148 consecutive games. He is so dependable, in fact, that when he lay on the turf clutching his knee during a game against Baltimore in 1996, it was more than worrisome to his teammates. It was downright frightening.

"I almost had a heart attack," said Erric Pegram, who was a Steelers' running back at the time. "It was a horrible nightmare, like Amityville Horror, Jason, and Friday the Thirteenth all mixed up into one thing."

The nightmare ended three plays later when Dawson jogged back onto the field. He also hurt his head and his ribs that season, but he never left the lineup. So how does he do it? How does he avoid debilitating injury while those around him are fitted for casts and crutches?

"Just divine intervention and a little luck," Dawson says with a smile.

John Elway

Denver Broncos

Rarely has a person's image changed so dramatically on one afternoon. Before Super Bowl XXXII, a nation of sports fans knew John Elway as a gifted quarterback and an indefatigable competitor, but one who was destined for defeat in football's ultimate game.

It was almost fun to feel sorry for the guy with the penetrating blue eyes and the toothy grin. He cut short the pitying sighs, however, when he led his Denver Broncos to a 31-24 upset of Green Bay. Now the three Super Bowl losses (XXI, XXII, and XXIV) seem easily explained by the lack of talent assembled around him in Denver. During Elway's 15-year career, his offensive linemen and wide receivers have been voted to the Pro Bowl a total of only seven times.

"There's a reason he was always making those come-from-behind victories," tight end Shannon Sharpe says. "We were always behind."

Elway's reversal of fortune came when his former quarterbacks coach and offensive coordinator, Mike Shanahan, returned to Denver as head coach in 1995. Rarely have a coach and his field general been more compatible. The addition of running back Terrell Davis opened up Elway's options and helped the Broncos post the AFC's best record (13-3)

in 1996. Elway's numbers have soared, taking him to second place all-time in completions (3,913) and passing yards (48,669).

Now that the question—"Will Elway ever win the big one?"—has been answered, his place in NFL history has become the hot topic.

"If you built a prototype quarterback, it would be John," says Jim Fassel, coach of the New York Giants who coached Elway at both Stanford and Denver. "He is the essence of a quarterback."

His physical abilities are legendary. As long-time CBS and FOX announcer Pat Summerall once said, "John Elway is the master of the inconceivable pass thrown to the unreachable spot."

His teammates talk about the Elway Cross, a small mark known to appear when one of his

> "If you built a prototype quarterback, it would be John. He is the essence of a quarterback."
> — Jim Fassel

leather bullets strikes a receiver nose-to-skin. Former Broncos cornerback Wymon Henderson once wandered in front of a practice pass by Elway, and the ball wound up lodged in his facemask. On one of Elway's first dates with his college sweetheart and future wife, Janet, the two were playing catch with a football. She told him to fire one, and Elway broke her pinkie finger.

He is, in fact, a superior all-around athlete. He hit .349 and had 50 RBI in 49 games as a sopho-

more at Stanford, and was drafted by two Major League teams. He is a 1-handicap golfer, a ferocious Ping-Pong player, and a reliable punter when called upon.

And few quarterbacks ever have run better. Elway has more carries than any quarterback in history, and his uncanny aptitude for scrambling out of traffic (he claims to use both sounds and shadows) has driven many an NFL pass rusher crazy. "His ability to make off-schedule plays, I think, has defined his career," says Gary Kubiak, who backed up Elway for nine seasons and now serves as his offensive coordinator.

Perhaps it is this talent for improvisation that has cemented Elway's reputation as the quarterback who refuses to lose. It isn't just the fact that he has won more games (138) than any other passer in history. It is the way he has done it, so

often untying his team from the railroad tracks just before the locomotive comes roaring past.

Elway's most famous miracle came in the 1986 AFC Championship Game, when he took the Broncos 98 yards in 15 plays to tie the Browns with 39 seconds left at Cleveland. (Denver then won 23-20 in overtime.) They call that one "The Drive," but there have been so many others—45 game-saving drives in total, another NFL best. And the last one was the sweetest: a 5-play, 49-yard march that ended with Terrell Davis's touchdown plunge, which gave the Broncos that long-awaited Super Bowl triumph.

At the victory parade a week later, the Denver fans who have idolized Elway for so long (he gets about 40,000 letters per year) were out in force, their burdens finally lifted. "He is our friend, and he is our brother, and he is everything to us in Colorado," gushed one female admirer. "He's one in a million."

#7 JOHN ELWAY, Quarterback

YEAR	TEAM	ATT	COMP	PCT	YDS	TD	INT	RATING
1983	Denver	259	123	47.5	1,663	7	14	54.9
1984	Denver	380	214	56.3	2,598	18	15	76.8
1985	Denver	605	327	54.1	3,891	22	23	70.2
1986	Denver	504	280	55.6	3,485	19	13	79.0
1987	Denver	410	224	54.6	3,198	19	12	83.4
1988	Denver	496	274	55.2	3,309	17	19	71.4
1989	Denver	416	223	53.6	3,051	18	18	73.7
1990	Denver	502	294	58.6	3,526	15	14	78.5
1991	Denver	451	242	53.7	3,253	13	12	75.4
1992	Denver	316	174	55.1	2,242	10	17	65.7
1993	Denver	551	348	63.2	4,030	25	10	92.8
1994	Denver	494	307	62.2	3,490	16	10	85.7
1995	Denver	542	316	58.3	3,970	26	14	86.4
1996	Denver	466	287	61.6	3,328	26	14	89.2
1997	Denver	502	280	55.8	3,635	27	11	87.5
CAREER TOTALS		6,894	3,913	56.8	48,669	278	216	79.2

Brett Favre

Green Bay Packers

Brett Favre is the only player who could share the NFL most-valuable-player award and consider it a disappointment. Actually, Favre had nothing but good things to say about tying Detroit running back Barry Sanders for the most votes in 1997. But it was a slight backslide for the man who had won the 1995 and 1996 awards outright.

As it is, Favre is the only three-time winner of the *Associated Press* NFL MVP award. And he probably will be fighting for the award again in 1998.

Any way you measure it, he is the yardstick for NFL dominance. You can begin with a throwing arm as strong as any in the league. His mother, Bonita, remembers a fifth-grade basketball game in which Brett launched a desperation heave the length of the court; it hit the far wall of the gym so hard that it knocked a fire extinguisher to the floor and broke it. At the NFL Quarterback Challenge in Hawaii one year, Favre launched a 79-yard pass—into a stiff breeze.

"He makes throws that other quarterbacks wouldn't dare," Packers head coach Mike Holmgren says. "He can throw with terrific velocity even when he is in quite awkward positions."

But a strong arm will take an NFL quarterback only so far. Favre stands apart because he also happens to be one of the game's most

intense competitors. It is a quality that naturally rubs off on his teammates.

"When you watch him play," says Packers general manager Ron Wolf, the man who got Favre in a 1992 trade with the Atlanta Falcons, "I don't think you ever have the feeling that his team is out of the game. It's like they'd always say about [Detroit's] Bobby Layne: He never lost a game; the clock just ran out on him."

Over the last three seasons, the clock hasn't run

out on Favre very often. His Packers are 44-13 during that period, including a victory over the Patriots in Super Bowl XXXI. And always at the center of attention is the boyish passer with the Huck Finn freckles.

"Last year we saw [Buccaneers defensive tackle] Warren Sapp and Brett Favre jawing at each other in the playoffs," former NFL wide receiver James Lofton says. "Here was a quarterback who not only had the respect of his teammates, but also the respect of the most vaunted player on the other side. Sapp was admitting that the only way his team could win was not to shut down the run or put on a strong rush, but to get inside the mind of Brett

> "Brett is one of the toughest guys on the team," wide receiver Robert Brooks says. "To know that your leader can endure punishment and not miss games— that he'll be there all the time—gives you a sense of confidence."

Favre and take him out of his game." It didn't work. It rarely does.

Mentally and physically, Favre is as rugged as a quarterback gets. Before his senior season at Southern Mississippi a car accident left him with a concussion, a cracked vertebra, and 30 fewer inches of intestine; five weeks later, he led the Golden Eagles to an upset victory at Alabama. He threw 5 touchdown passes against Chicago while playing with torn ankle ligaments in 1995, and he completed 23 of 33 passes with a separated left shoulder to help upset the Eagles in 1992. He enters the 1998 season with 93 consecutive starts in regular-season

games, far and away the most in the league.

"Brett is one of the toughest guys on the team," wide receiver Robert Brooks says. "To know that your leader can endure punishment and not miss games—that he'll be there all the time—gives you a sense of confidence."

It also helps when he's putting points on the board, and nobody does that better than Favre. In 1997, he became the first NFL quarterback ever to log four consecutive 30-touchdown seasons. (He had a league-high 35 to go with his second-best 3,867 passing yards.) He had 39 scoring passes in 1996 and 38 in 1995, the third- and fourth-best season totals ever. After only six seasons in Green Bay, he owns club records for attempts (3,201), completions (1,971), and touchdown passes (182).

Favre seems to make everything look easy. In fact, about the only thing he finds difficult is dealing with celebrity. He sees himself as just an excitable country boy from Kiln, Mississippi, population 50. He still walks around with a stubbled chin, in a baggy sweatshirt. He still enjoys nothing more than fishing or playing golf. He can't help it if he happens to be one of the best athletes on the planet.

#4 BRETT FAVRE, Quarterback

YEAR	TEAM	ATT	COMP	PCT	YDS	TD	INT	RATING
1991	Atlanta	5	0	0.0	0	0	2	0.0
1992	Green Bay	471	302	64.1	3,227	18	13	85.3
1993	Green Bay	522	318	60.9	3,303	19	24	72.2
1994	Green Bay	582	363	62.4	3,882	33	14	90.7
1995	Green Bay	570	359	63.0	4,413	38	13	99.5
1996	Green Bay	543	325	59.9	3,899	39	13	95.8
1997	Green Bay	513	304	59.3	3,867	35	16	92.6
CAREER TOTALS		3,206	1,971	61.5	22,591	182	95	89.3

Eddie George

Sometimes, mother really does know best. If it weren't for Donna George's perceptiveness, who knows what would have become of her son, Eddie? It is highly unlikely he would have developed into a Pro Bowl running back.

Eddie George grew up in Philadelphia, which he describes as "hard-core and hard-nosed, a rough city, a blue-collar city." It was all of that for Eddie, and he wasn't helping matters with his attitude, or with the friends he kept.

"We'd do things like staying out late, drinking, gambling, and basically just being a menace to society," he says.

Donna had seen enough. She decided Eddie needed more structure in his life—and this was a unilateral decision. There was no debate, no show of hands. She helped him pack his bags, and off he went to Fork Union Military Academy in Virginia.

Fork Union was no picnic. It is a place where students have to rise at dawn, turn lights out by 10 P.M., and grunt through a lot of chores in between. It also happens to have a respected football program that already had produced Vinny Testaverde and Don Majkowski, a couple of future NFL quarterbacks.

"My mom sending me to the academy changed my attitude and my life," George says.

The rewards were not immediate, however. After an unspectacular senior season, George received no interest from the nation's college football programs. So he took matters into his own hands. He found a directory of universities and made so many phone calls that his fingers hurt from punching buttons. The result? Zip. Not an offer.

George went back to Fork Union for a postgraduate year and rejoined the football team. He was declared ineligible after half a season, but that was all he needed to show his full package of skills. This time the college recruiters came out of the woodwork.

"I can't do what every man does," George says. "I have to do something extra."

George chose Ohio State, and in his freshman year he became one of the most recognizable players on the team. Unfortunately, it was because he fumbled twice at the goal line in a loss to Illinois. "I was the most hated person on campus," George says.

He had come too far to get bogged down by one game, though. George earned a starting role as a junior. And by the time he left Columbus he was

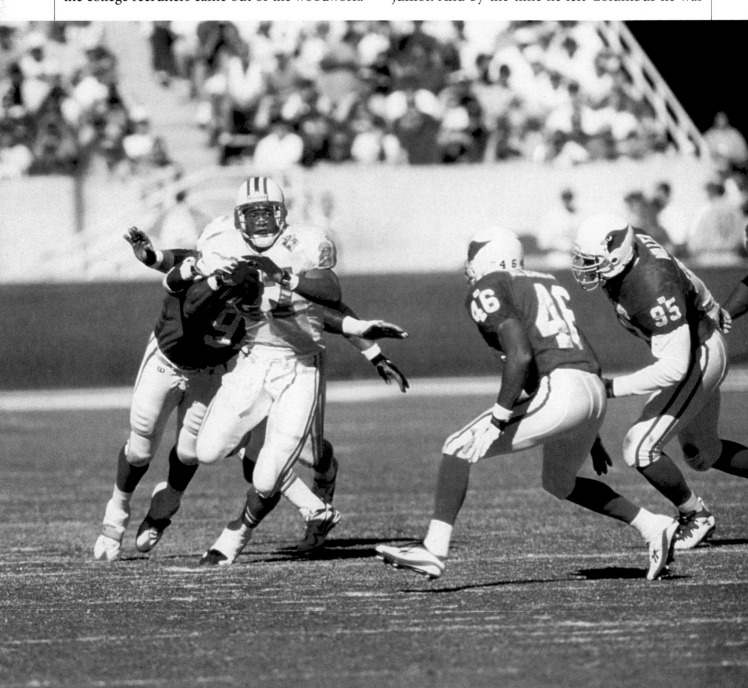

carrying the 1995 Heisman Trophy. He won the award after setting school records for rushing yards in a season (1,927) and a game (314 against Illinois), while scoring 25 touchdowns.

George's pace barely has slackened in the NFL. He ranked third in the AFC, fifth in the NFL, in each of his first two seasons, rushing for 1,368 yards in 1996 and 1,399 in 1997. They were the two most productive seasons ever for an Oilers' running back not named Earl Campbell. And his two-year total of 2,767 is the fifth best ever for a runner in his first two NFL seasons. It is the man at the top of that list to whom George is most often compared.

"He kind of reminds me of Eric Dickerson because he is big, strong, and powerful," Bills running back Thurman Thomas says.

A lot of 250-pound fullbacks are big and powerful. What puts the 6-foot 3-inch, 232-pound George in the category of Dickerson is his breakaway speed. "He can do both," agreed Barry Sanders, generally considered the game's best running back. "He can cut and slash, and he can bruise you by running hard."

In his rookie season George broke a 76-yard run at Jacksonville, the Oilers' longest in 13 years. Guys who weigh 232 pounds aren't supposed to do that. In the opening game of 1997, he cut, slashed, and bruised the Raiders for 216 yards, which tied Billy Cannon's club record.

George's exploits are the extension of his ceaseless drive. When an Oilers' practice ends, it usually is just halftime for the muscled runner, who is known to put in an extra two to three hours of sweat. Most days he begins his post-practice workout with eight full-speed, 60-yard sprints, then heads to the weight room for a grueling workout.

"Eddie is a workhorse," Oilers quarterback Steve McNair says. "That helps him be a better player because as the third and fourth quarter goes on and everyone else gets tired, he gets going."

That's one reason George labors so hard. A deeper explanation is that about eight years ago he started pushing himself as far as he could go, and now he doesn't know how to stop.

"I can't do what every man does," George says. "I have to do something extra."

#27 EDDIE GEORGE, Running Back

| YEAR | TEAM | RUSHING | | | | RECEIVING | | | |
		NO	YDS	AVG	TD	NO	YDS	AVG	TD
1996	Houston	335	1,368	4.1	8	23	182	7.9	0
1997	Tennessee	357	1,399	3.9	6	7	44	6.3	1
CAREER TOTALS		692	2,767	4.0	14	30	226	7.5	1

Merton Hanks

San Francisco 49ers

In December, 1997, Merton Hanks went to Collins Elementary School in Cupertino, California, as part of the NFL's Take a Player to School program. The 49ers' Pro Bowl free safety patiently fulfilled every request made of him that day, except one: He wouldn't do the dance.

"I don't do that without warming up," said Hanks with a smile.

Some people have taken to calling it the Chicken Dance, but Hanks never officially has applied a name to what he does after making a game-saving play. You've probably seen it before: He intercepts a last-second pass in the end zone or scoops up a fumble and runs it back for a touchdown. Then his bones go rubbery and his body convulses as if charged with an electric current. The crowd either hisses or cheers wildly, depending on where it is taking place.

The dance is what fans most closely identify with Hanks, but it is the play preceding it that his teammates usually remember.

Though he was an All–Big Ten cornerback at Iowa (and despite the fact that he was a district champion in the 110-meter hurdles at Lake Highlands High School in Dallas), the 40-yard dashes he ran for NFL scouts were ruefully slow. The 49ers waited until the fifth round of the draft to take Hanks, and even then they had some misgivings.

Not only was he relatively lead-footed, his 6-foot 2-inch, 185-pound body looked as though it might break in a high-speed collision. His neck appears to be two times too long. But his coaches soon found that Hanks is a sponge when it comes to soaking up football knowledge. His film work and his on-field concentration are matched by only a few.

"When you're a fifth-round pick you don't get much leeway for mistakes," Hanks says. "On any given day they can send you home on a bus. You've got to fight for your job in every practice, every day. That's the mentality I picked up, and it's the one I have today. I still feel I have to justify my place on the field."

Hanks's place wasn't truly cemented until the fourth game of the 1993 season, when he filled in

for injured Dana Hall at free safety. Before that, Hanks had been an on-and-off starter at cornerback. But he was such a snug fit at safety, the 49ers had to wonder why they hadn't put him there all along. He engaged in one year of on-the-job training and was a Pro Bowl starter thereafter.

"Just look at his career," 49ers defensive coordinator John Marshall says. "He's a big-play guy."

Big plays? Hanks has returned only 2 punts in his seven-year career; one of them was a 48-yard touchdown at Atlanta in 1992. He set a school record at Iowa with 7 blocked kicks. More significant are his takeaways. Hanks is a reflexive ballhawk who often steps in front of a pass before the wide receiver even knows it is coming. With a team-high 6 interceptions in 1997, he has 22 over the last four seasons. That total ranks second in the NFL to Aeneas Williams's 27. Hanks also has 5 fumble recoveries in that

span, not to mention innumerable crucial tackles.

The play of the 49ers' safeties—strong safety Tim McDonald is a six-time Pro Bowl selection—makes things easier for the entire defense, which ranked first in the NFL last year.

"For the corners, you can do so much back there when you've got someone like Merton," cornerback Darnell Walker says. "You can take some chances. You've got to know who you're playing with—and he's an awesome player."

When Hanks gets on a roll, no free ball is safe. Last November he hurt his hand against Dallas. The cast he wore over the next three weeks must have included a small nuclear generator because he clearly was energized. At Philadelphia he picked up Ricky Watters's fumble and took it 38 yards for a touchdown on the second play of the game. Against Carolina a week later, he intercepted Kerry Collins's pass at the goal line to end the game and clinch the NFC West title. And a week after that he set up 10 points with 2 interceptions against San Diego's Craig Whelihan.

After the second interception against the Chargers, a nice read that set up a short touchdown drive, Hanks could contain himself no longer. He started trembling, and soon he was shaking like the epicenter of an 8.0 earthquake.

This time, he had warmed up for the act.

#36 MERTON HANKS, Safety

YEAR	TEAM	TACKLES	SACKS	FUM REC	INT	YDS	AVG	TD
1991	San Francisco	37	0.0	2	0	0	—	0
1992	San Francisco	64	0.0	0	2	5	2.5	0
1993	San Francisco	71	0.0	1	3	104	34.7	1
1994	San Francisco	79	0.5	1	7	93	13.3	0
1995	San Francisco	72	0.0	2	5	31	6.2	0
1996	San Francisco	80	0.0	0	4	7	1.8	0
1997	San Francisco	86	0.0	2	6	103	17.2	1
CAREER TOTALS		489	0.5	8	27	343	12.7	2

Levon Kirkland

Somewhere in the bowels of Three Rivers Stadium there must be a top-secret laboratory that manufactures Pro Bowl linebackers. Because no matter how many the Steelers lose, they seem to be able to produce replacements.

First it was Hardy Nickerson, on the verge of stardom, who bolted to Tampa Bay as a free agent in 1993. In 1996 the Steelers were doubly depleted: pass rusher Kevin Greene signed with Carolina, then Greg Lloyd, one of the most intimidating players in the game, suffered a season-ending knee injury. That opened the door for young Chad Brown, but he, too, was gone a year later, to Seattle.

Yet the Pittsburgh defense has continued to thrive in the wake of the defections. And the biggest reason may be the guy with the biggest jersey number: 99, Levon Kirkland.

Kirkland has been to the last two Pro Bowls, and a play he made against Buffalo in 1996 suggests why. Driving in Steelers' territory, Bills quarterback Jim Kelly spotted tight end Lonnie Johnson breaking open over the middle. He lofted a pass, only to see Kirkland make a diving, over-the-shoulder, one-handed catch for an interception.

"Unbelievable play," Steelers director of team operations Tom Donahoe said afterward. "I thought he was beat. I'm sure Kelly did, too."

It was the kind of catch you would expect from Cris Carter or Herman Moore, not from a man built like a nose tackle. Kirkland stands 6 feet 1 inch and weighs 264 pounds, but it's hard to believe it when you see him move.

"He's a freak," Donahoe says. "It's not like you look at the guy and say he's heavy or fat. He's big,

thick, and can run. Physically he's awesome. He can just blow plays up."

"He does everything a receiver or a running back can do," Pittsburgh linebacker Earl Holmes says. "People think because he's big like that, he can't run. But we see it. He can run."

That's not the only way in which Kirkland's looks are deceptive. With his wire-rimmed spectacles and pensive gaze, the preacher's son from Lamar, South Carolina (the town of 1,300 where he still lives), appears to be a solemn man. Don't believe it. He reads comic books by the dozen, and he broke up the entire Steelers' locker room a couple years ago with an imitation of head coach Bill Cowher.

"I like to have fun," Kirkland says. "I like to cut

up. If you look at me from a distance and did not know me, I'm wearing glasses and not smiling…I'm a big guy. People think I'm serious. The only time I'm serious is when I play football."

And then he is a serious problem for NFL offenses. Kirkland is one of those rare players who is both explosive and steady. On the one hand, he seems to have a knack for coming up big in crucial situations. In 1993, his first year as a starter, he preserved a 17-14 victory by stopping New England's Drew Bledsoe on a goal-line plunge. And there are many who feel Kirkland was the most valuable player of Super Bowl XXX. He roamed the field for 10 tackles, including a sack, but the Steelers came up short against Dallas.

On the other hand, Kirkland consistently is effective. He hasn't missed a game in six NFL seasons, and since moving into the starting lineup he has been the team's leading or second-leading tackler every year. He is a team captain (they call him Captain Kirk), and he calls the Steelers' defensive signals.

"He takes pride in getting people lined up, and has really assumed a leadership role in our defense," head coach Bill Cowher says. "His development has made him an integral part of what we do."

Kirkland still is adding new facets to his game. When Lloyd went down in 1996, Kirkland replaced him in Pittsburgh's Nickel and Dime packages. Lloyd returned in 1997, but by midseason Kirkland had regained his spot as a pass defender and wound up with a career-high 5 sacks while the defense improved markedly.

You might say he grew into the job, just as he grew into his body after going to Clemson as a 205-pound outside linebacker. It is said that Kirkland played some games at 277 pounds last year. That might make him the largest linebacker ever to play in the NFL. Soon, he might be considered one of the best.

#99 LEVON KIRKLAND, Linebacker

YEAR	TEAM	TACKLES	SACKS	FUM REC	INT	YDS	AVG	TD
1992	Pittsburgh	5	0.0	0	0	0	—	0
1993	Pittsburgh	103	1.0	2	0	0	—	0
1994	Pittsburgh	100	3.0	0	2	0	0.0	0
1995	Pittsburgh	88	1.0	2	0	0	—	0
1996	Pittsburgh	113	4.0	0	4	12	3.0	0
1997	Pittsburgh	126	5.0	1	2	14	7.0	0
CAREER TOTALS		535	14.0	5	8	26	3.3	0

Dorsey Levens

Dorsey Levens is more than a starting running back to Packers head coach Mike Holmgren; he's a personal talisman. Holmgren used Levens to scare away the only two demons that remained to haunt his successful NFL career: Dallas and Minnesota.

Holmgren had an embarrassing 0-7 record against the Cowboys when the two teams prepared to meet last season. Desperately searching for an answer, he was told that Green Bay had averaged a paltry 58.1 rushing yards in the seven games against Dallas. So he gave to ball to Levens, again and again, and, at the end, the relatively unheralded runner had carried 33 times for 190 yards, breaking Jim Taylor's 36-year-old club record of 186. And Green Bay earned a 45-17 victory.

"That's the hardest running I've seen out there since Taylor," said legendary Packers linebacker Ray Nitschke.

A week later, the Packers traveled to the Metrodome in Minneapolis, where Holmgren was 0-5 since taking charge of the team in 1992. Levens was a marked man this time, but he fought for 108 yards on 31 attempts, helping Green Bay to a liberating 27-11 win.

By the end of the season, Holmgren's good-luck charm had run for 1,435 yards, second best in the NFC (behind Barry Sanders) and only 39 yards shy of Taylor's club record. According to his workmates, no one deserved the strong season more than Levens.

"He's as humble a guy as you're ever going to meet," says Harry Sydney, Green Bay's running backs coach.

Of course, until his breakthrough season Levens had good reason to be humble. The victim of more bad breaks than the villain in a Jackie Chan movie, his path to stardom was filled with obstacles.

After a stellar high school career in Syracuse, New York, Levens set

"To be honest with you," Green Bay offensive coordinator Sherman Lewis would say later, "I don't think we thought he was as good as he is."

off for Notre Dame, where he promptly encountered obstacle number one: a stable of backs that included Ricky Watters, Jerome Bettis, Rodney Culver, Reggie Brooks, and Anthony Johnson—all of them destined for the NFL. But Levens was up to the challenge, and after rushing for 200 yards in the spring game he was handed the starting tailback job in 1990. Unfortunately, he injured

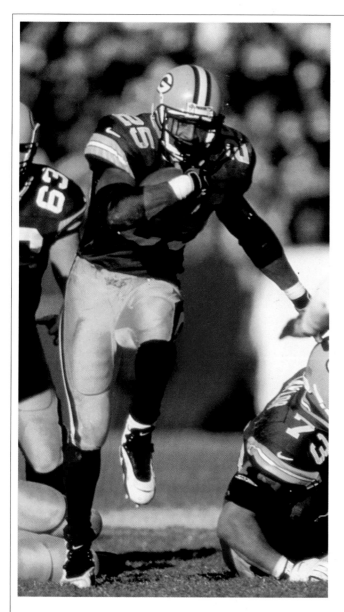

ing primarily in a one-back set on passing downs. It was an unglamorous job, but Levens played so efficiently that the Packers had no choice but to increase his action. He was brilliant in the 1996 postseason, killing Carolina's hopes in the NFC Championship Game (205 yards from scrimmage) and turning in a game-high 61 yards rushing against New England in Super Bowl XXXI.

Determined to win a first-string assignment, Levens quickly embarked on a tough offseason exercise program under the watchful eye of former LSU women's track coach Loren Seagrave. The workouts included stadium steps, cone drills, abdominal work, and sets of 100-yard sprints followed by pushups or situps.

As it turned out, Levens needed the conditioning. Bennett went down with a ruptured Achilles tendon in the preseason, and Levens was given the full-time job. He never gave it back.

Levens still appears to be caught between positions at times. He isn't blazingly fast, nor immensely strong. But he has the moves to get past the line of scrimmage and he can break tackles in the open field. He also is a reliable ball handler who went 180 consecutive carries without a fumble last year. In short, he's a perfect fit for the Packers' intricate offense.

"I judge our running backs on not only the yards that they gain," Holmgren says, "but [whether] they are doing a good job picking up blitzes. They have to be able to block. Are they catching passes in our passing game?

"Dorsey is doing all those things."

At least one long-time observer is not surprised. "Dorsey has always put 150 percent into everything he does," says his mother, Pat.

his knee before the season started. The next year he transferred to Georgia Tech, where he had a couple of good years but didn't set the collegiate world on fire.

So Levens was a marginal pick in the 1994 draft, and his stock didn't rise any when ESPN's self-appointed "draft guru," Mel Kiper, Jr., called him the most overrated player on the board. The Packers finally selected him in the fifth round.

"To be honest with you," Green Bay offensive coordinator Sherman Lewis would say later, "I don't think we thought he was as good as he is."

Levens didn't get to prove himself right away, either. He started at fullback in 1995, but lost his job to William Henderson in '96. He spent most of that season behind halfback Edgar Bennett, play-

#25 DORSEY LEVENS, Running Back

YEAR	TEAM	RUSHING				RECEIVING			
		NO	YDS	AVG	TD	NO	YDS	AVG	TD
1994	Green Bay	5	15	3.0	0	1	9	9.0	0
1995	Green Bay	36	120	3.3	3	48	434	9.0	4
1996	Green Bay	121	566	4.7	5	31	226	7.3	5
1997	Green Bay	329	1,435	4.4	7	53	370	7.0	5
CAREER TOTALS		491	2,136	4.4	15	133	1,039	7.8	14

Dan Marino 13

Miami Dolphins

When you talk about Dan Marino, the numbers start to fall like hail. During his 15-year NFL career Marino has set so many major passing records that his write-up in the Miami Dolphins' media guide is longer than some pulp romance novels.

To begin with, Marino is the NFL's all-time leader in attempts (7,452 entering the 1998 season), completions (4,453), passing yards (55,416), and touchdown passes (385). He reached 30,000 yards and 40,000 yards faster than any other quarterback, and he is the only one yet to surpass 50,000. He has completed passes to 69 different players, from Mark Duper and Mark Clayton to Joe Rose, Irving Spikes, and even Dan Marino (after a pass was batted by an opponent). He has thrown touchdown passes to 48 different players—including 79 to former wide receiver Clayton—in 33 different stadiums. He is the only quarterback in NFL history to post six 4,000-yard seasons, and only he and John Elway have recorded 3,000 yards in 12 different seasons.

He owns league records with 56 career 300-yard games and 20 games with 4 touchdown passes, and last year he had his record streak of 13 consecutive postseason games with a touchdown pass snapped by the Patriots. He never has gone three consecutive games without a touchdown pass. In 1997, at a time when some claimed he had lost it, he set a Dolphins' record by throwing 156 consecutive passes without an interception while posting the NFL's sixth-highest passer rating. He also has played in more regular-season games (215) in more seasons (16, including this year) than any other Miami player. In 1983, he set an NFL rookie record with a passer rating of 96.0.

"Nobody likes to have their records broken, but I'm very proud to have Danny break them," says Fran Tarkenton, who watched his major career marks tumble in 1995. "Nobody's played the game any better than Dan Marino. And I don't think, by the time he's done, that anybody will break those records in his lifetime."

Maybe by the time he's done we'll have figured out how he did it. Marino is big (6 feet 4 inches, 228 pounds), but some quarterbacks can throw

the ball farther. He's never been much of a runner. And the Dolphins rarely have had a running game to support him.

But Len Dawson, the former NFL quarterback who now hosts a football show for HBO, has an explanation. "The one thing about Dan Marino that stands out, no matter what his physical condition might be, is his competitiveness," Dawson says. "He is one of those players who believes he's never out of it."

Most of the time he isn't. Marino's record as a starter is 132-81; without him the Dolphins are 8-10. Other observers point to his active mind for the game, and what might be the quickest throwing motion ever seen. As former teammate Jim Jensen says of Marino's delivery: "He sees it; it's gone. There's no thinking."

But that's too easy, according to Don Shula. "Everybody talks about Dan's quick release," says Shula, his coach for 13 seasons. "The things that people don't talk about much are his abilities to make quick decisions and to sense when defenders are closing in on him."

"Nobody likes to have their records broken, but I'm very proud to have Danny break them," says Fran Tarkenton.

Perhaps that is why the lumbering Marino has been sacked so few times in his career. In 1988, remarkably, he was sacked only 6 times while attempting 606 passes. And that, in turn, is part of why he has proved so durable. Despite numerous operations, Marino has suffered only one major injury: a torn Achilles tendon that knocked him out of 11 games in 1993 and still prevents him from rising up on his right toes without support. Before that setback he had started 145 consecutive games.

Despite Marino's individual accolades, though, a Super Bowl victory has eluded him. He made it to Super Bowl XIX in only his second season, but lost to the 49ers and has never returned. As his career winds down, he now must face the possibility of leaving the sport without a championship. Believe it or not, he isn't all that worried about getting a ring.

"You've got to have dreams," Marino says. "But I can look back at my career knowing I worked for that goal each and every year, and I don't think it will take away from my career if I don't get one."

#13 DAN MARINO, Quarterback

YEAR	TEAM	ATT	COMP	PCT	YDS	TD	INT	RATING
1983	Miami	296	173	58.5	2,210	20	6	96.0
1984	Miami	564	362	64.2	5,084	48	17	108.9
1985	Miami	567	336	59.3	4,137	30	21	84.1
1986	Miami	623	378	60.7	4,746	44	23	92.5
1987	Miami	444	263	59.2	3,245	26	13	89.2
1988	Miami	606	354	58.4	4,434	28	23	80.8
1989	Miami	550	308	56.0	3,997	24	22	76.9
1990	Miami	531	306	57.6	3,563	21	11	82.6
1991	Miami	549	318	57.9	3,970	25	13	85.8
1992	Miami	554	330	59.6	4,116	24	16	85.1
1993	Miami	150	91	60.7	1,218	8	3	95.9
1994	Miami	615	385	62.6	4,453	30	17	89.2
1995	Miami	482	309	64.1	3,668	24	15	90.8
1996	Miami	373	221	59.2	2,795	17	9	87.8
1997	Miami	548	319	58.2	3,780	16	11	80.7
CAREER TOTALS		7,452	4,453	59.8	55,416	385	220	87.8

Bruce Matthews

Tennessee Oilers

As far as the Tennessee Oilers are concerned, cloning technology is being refined a few decades too late. If only it were up and running now, Bruce Matthews might be the NFL's answer to Dolly the sheep. The Oilers would love having five of him to open holes and protect the passer.

Matthews has started at all five offensive line positions during his career. We're not talking about token appearances, either. He has started 74 games at center, 67 games at right guard, 48 at left guard (his latest post), 22 at right tackle, and 17 at left tackle—at least a full 16-game season at each. His 10 Pro Bowl selections include honors at all three interior positions. Matthews also is the team's long snapper for field goals and extra points.

"To have the ability to be flexible and dominate wherever you play is invaluable," New York Jets defensive coordinator Bill Belichick says. "What more could you ask of a player? Sell refreshments?"

Matthews would probably win Salesman of the Month. Versatility is nothing new to this guy. He was a prep All-America as both an offensive and defensive lineman at Arcadia High School in suburban Los Angeles. He also was a two-time all-league wrestler. At the University of Southern California, he filled all five offensive line spots at various times, earning consensus All-America honors at guard as a senior.

The Oilers, then in Houston, took him with the ninth pick in the 1983 draft, and Matthews has been starting ever since. One of his teammates in '83 was defensive end Elvin Bethea, who established club records by playing in 210 games over 16 seasons. Bethea passed the torch to Matthews, who broke the record by playing in 232 games by the end of 1997. Matthews now is in his sixteenth season, too. His active run of 165 consecutive starts (entering 1998) is the longest streak in the NFL at any position—and he had to play through a painful knee injury last season to keep it alive.

If the 6-foot 5-inch, 298-pound lineman's tenacity is hard to fathom, you must consider the values instilled by his father, Clay Matthews, Sr.

"I told all of them, 'You can go play any sport

you want to,'" Clay, Sr., says. "'But there are two rules. One of them is, I don't care if you're last string and sit on the bench all the time and you're the worst guy out there—you can't quit. Number two, if I ever see you play or practice and you're not giving it 120 percent of what you've got, I'm going to yank you out of there myself.'"

Dad wasn't barking empty words. His own determination allowed him to play four seasons as an end with the 49ers in the 1950s. And Bruce wasn't the only one listening. His older brother, Clay, Jr., played 19 seasons as a linebacker with the Browns and Falcons. They were teammates in two Pro Bowls.

Of the brothers, Bruce is probably dominant.

> "Teams plan their defenses to stay away from [Bruce] Matthews," says Belichick.

"Teams plan their defenses to stay away from [Bruce] Matthews," says Belichick, who believes the guard has been worthy of MVP consideration. "He is one of the few offensive linemen who can check the player in front of him and also pick up a blitzing cornerback or linebacker coming from the outside."

As Chargers linebacker Junior Seau says, "Matthews is going to know every move you make. Hopefully he'll make a false step, which he rarely does, and you can get by him."

Off the field, Matthews is just as steady. He holds a degree in industrial engineering. His favorite book is the Bible. He is a retiring man who relishes domestic life. "My entertainment and

leisure time is spent playing with my four boys and girl [ages 4 to 13]," Matthews says. "Our existence is defined by our children."

That existence caught some minor turbulence when the Oilers moved from Houston to Memphis in 1997, just after the family had finished building a new home. Then again, change is not something that throws Bruce off balance. Besides all those position switches, he has powered offenses that ranged from the wide-open run-and-shoot to Tennessee's current attack, built around the hard running of Eddie George.

In an ever-changing game, it's helpful to have a few constants on which to rely. One of them is Bruce Matthews, still a pillar at the age of 37.

"I still feel like a kid," he says. "Then I look at the age and birth dates and realize that when I was in high school, a lot of these guys were being born."

Warren Moon

Seattle Seahawks

The Seattle Seahawks acquired Warren Moon as a safety net in 1997. They wanted a quarterback to provide veteran leadership in the locker room, to take a few snaps when needed. The Seahawks should have known better. We all should have known better.

Warren Moon, who usually ends up in the spotlight, ended up in the spotlight.

When starter John Friesz broke his thumb in the first game, Moon suddenly had the starting job. By season's end, the man with the picture-perfect spiral had shattered Seattle club season records for passing yards (3,678) and completions (313). He sparked the NFL's top-rated passing offense, played in his ninth Pro Bowl, and wound up being named MVP of the game. Not bad for a guy who turned 41 midway through the season.

If Moon is the Ponce de Leon of the National Football League, his Fountain of Youth springs from an ardent commitment to conditioning and practice. Moon has kept his skill level amazingly high as his contemporaries have succumbed to retirement. Last year he became the oldest NFL player ever to pass for 400 yards (409) and 5 touchdowns in a game (versus the Raiders on October 26), and the oldest ever to score a touchdown (at Indianapolis on September 14).

Sometimes the whole senior citizen

angle is too much for the charismatic passer. "It gets a little old," Moon says. "I think some of my ability and some of my skills get lost in the fact that I'm forty."

And yet, his endurance is hard to discount. "A lot of times when I'm talking to Warren," says Joey

Galloway, the Seahawks' star wide receiver, "I almost want to call him Mr. Moon out of respect for what he's done."

He has done plenty. Moon is the only quarterback ever to play in eight consecutive Pro Bowls (following the 1988–95 seasons). He holds the single-season passing record not only for the Seahawks, but also for the Oilers (4,690 in 1991) and Vikings (4,264 in 1994). He owns the NFL's second-best one-game passing mark, 527 yards against an excellent Kansas City defense in 1990. (Norm Van Brocklin's enduring record of 554 yards in 1951 was set against the New York Yanks, who finished 1-9-2.) Moon enters the 1998 season ranked third in NFL history with 47,465 passing yards, fourth with 279 touchdowns.

Imagine what he might have accomplished had he not spent six seasons north of the 48th parallel. Undrafted out of college—despite leading the University of Washington to a Rose Bowl victory in 1978—Moon signed with the Edmonton Eskimos of the Canadian Football League. There he helped the team to five Grey Cup titles and passed for 21,228 yards.

If Moon took an arduous route to NFL stardom, first signing with the Oilers in 1984, it is wholly appropriate. This is no devil-may-care free spirit along the lines of Bobby Layne or Brett Favre. Moon barely had started elementary school when his father died, and he remembers his mother telling him at the time, "You're the man of the house now." (He has five siblings, all sisters.)

So young Harold Warren Moon learned responsibility, and he never has forgotten it. He is the perfect

corporate quarterback, a guy who usually brings a quarterbacks coach, a strength coach, and a video man out with him on the first day of workouts, so that he can dissect any budding mechanical problems.

"In agent selection he talked to sportswriters, coaches, clients of mine," says Leigh Steinberg, who got the job 20 years ago. "We probably talked on the phone twenty-five or thirty times before he made his choice."

Moon has taken this boardroom approach off the field, too. He is part-owner of a real-estate development company and a producer of health products and cosmetics. He also is one of the NFL's most involved community activists. In 1989, he set up the Crescent Moon Foundation to steer his educational projects, and it since has awarded more than 150 scholarships. He has assistants in two cities to help with the logistics.

Some have sized up Moon for a post-football political career. His articulate speech and movie-star looks make him a natural candidate for the broadcast booth, too. Then again, he's only 41 years old. Why look past the NFL?

"I know how I feel right now," Moon says. "I'm still having fun. I'm still enjoying it."

#1 WARREN MOON, Quarterback								
YEAR	TEAM	ATT	COMP	PCT	YDS	TD	INT	RATING
1984	Houston	450	259	57.6	3,338	12	14	76.9
1985	Houston	377	200	53.1	2,709	15	19	68.5
1986	Houston	488	256	52.5	3,489	13	26	62.3
1987	Houston	368	184	50.0	2,806	21	18	74.2
1988	Houston	294	160	54.4	2,327	17	8	88.4
1989	Houston	464	280	60.3	3,631	23	14	88.9
1990	Houston	584	362	62.0	4,689	33	13	96.8
1991	Houston	655	404	61.7	4,690	23	21	81.7
1992	Houston	346	224	64.7	2,521	18	12	89.3
1993	Houston	520	303	58.3	3,485	21	21	75.2
1994	Minnesota	601	371	61.7	4,264	18	19	79.9
1995	Minnesota	606	377	62.2	4,228	33	14	91.5
1996	Minnesota	247	134	54.3	1,610	7	9	68.7
1997	Seattle	528	313	59.3	3,678	25	16	83.7
CAREER TOTALS		6,528	3,827	58.6	47,465	279	224	81.2

Herman Moore

Herman Moore was destined to be a football star. He just had to experiment to find the right position.

His first try at George Washington High School in Danville, Virginia, was as a kicker. Moore actually set a school record with a 48-yard field goal, but his straight-on (non-soccer) style wouldn't have taken him very far. He caught a lot of passes as a senior, but mostly as a lanky tight end.

When Moore got to the University of Virginia, the coaches first tried him at defensive back. That experiment came to an end less than two weeks into preseason camp.

"I was playing free safety," Moore remembers, "and the fullback, Durwin Greggs, came through untouched. It was just me and him, and he ran me completely over. I reached to grab him and he never broke stride, just flattened me. That was my last play on defense."

As Moore lay on the turf, he probably wasn't dreaming about NFL stardom, but that is precisely what the future brought. After switching to offense and finding his position as a wide receiver, Moore set an NCAA record by catching touchdown passes in nine consecutive games as a junior. He joined the Lions as a first-round draft choice in 1991. He has maintained a similar pace in Detroit, and now holds club records for receptions (528 entering 1998), receiving yardage (7,484), and touchdown catches (52).

Moore is athletic and runs well after the catch, but he also is one of the best downfield blockers at his position. Already a head above the crowd of NFL defensive backs at 6 feet 4 inches, 210 pounds, he also is a great leaper. While his Virginia football teammates were enduring spring practice, Moore

was winning both indoor and outdoor titles in the high jump. His best indoor leap, 7 feet 2 ½ inches, established a school record.

But conversations with his coaches and teammates usually turn to his hands. Though not exceptionally large, they are powerful as vises. Moore does a lot of wrist curls, and grip work to keep his fingertips strong. One of his favorite exercises is taking an oval-shaped weight of one to three pounds and dropping it, then grabbing it before it hits the ground.

"I never learned to gather [the ball] in to my body," Moore says. "My security is catching it with my hands. If it's a play where I have to go low with my elbows on the ground, I'll still try to get my hands alone on the ball."

More often than not, he is successful. "With all due respect to the other fine receivers in this league," FOX analyst and former linebacker Matt Millen says, "Herman Moore has the best pure hands of any of them. They're like Venus-flytraps. They just suck in those passes."

Moore's combination of height, hands, and leaping ability makes him the ultimate posses-

> "With all due respect to the other fine receivers in this league, Herman Moore has the best pure hands of any of them. They're like Venus-flytraps. They just suck in those passes."
> — Matt Millen

sion receiver. Few players can reach as high; few balls escape his clutch.

He already had begun to show off his talents before 1995, but he joined the company of Jerry Rice and Michael Irvin in that breakthrough season. With Lions quarterback Scott Mitchell passing with regularity, Moore finished with an NFL-record 123 catches. His 1,686 yards were the fourth most in league history. And he hasn't slowed since. He finished second to Rice's 108 with 106 receptions in 1996 and tied Tim Brown for the NFL lead with 104 in 1997, becoming only the second player (Rice

being the other) to register three consecutive 100-catch seasons.

Don't expect the success to go to Moore's head. After signing a lucrative contract to begin his rookie NFL season, he and his wife Angela lived in a modest apartment and shared a pickup truck. When he showed up for his first preseason game, his wardrobe wasn't exactly from the Giorgio Armani collection.

"Man, did some of the other guys dog me!" Moore says. "I think the suit cost $129 at Sears. I had on $35 shoes."

Moore is one of Detroit's most popular athletes, a thoughtful, talkative guy who graduated with a bachelor's degree in rhetoric and communication studies. He also is a doting husband and father of two, and he and Angela are among the city's most visible spokespersons through Herman's Catch 84 Foundation.

"The attention I'm getting now means people might pay attention to some of the things I have to say," Moore says. "I talk to a lot of schools and community groups. We need people in the limelight to go out and get things across to young people, to help make things better for them."

#84 HERMAN MOORE, Wide Receiver

YEAR	TEAM	NO	YDS	AVG	TD
1991	Detroit	11	135	12.3	0
1992	Detroit	51	966	18.9	4
1993	Detroit	61	935	15.3	6
1994	Detroit	72	1,173	16.3	11
1995	Detroit	123	1,686	13.7	14
1996	Detroit	106	1,296	12.2	9
1997	Detroit	104	1,293	12.4	8
CAREER TOTALS		528	7,484	14.2	52

John Randle

Minnesota Vikings

Playing defensive tackle in the NFL is like slam-dancing in a pit full of grizzly bears. You are pummeled by offensive linemen, cut from the side by charging fullbacks, and sometimes nailed in the back by your own teammates. Most football players consider it the danger zone. But to Minnesota's John Randle, it's a piece of cake.

"In my life I've chopped cotton, picked watermelons, built fences, worked on an assembly line, worked in an oil field, built scaffolding," the five-time Pro Bowl defensive tackle says. "You know what? Those jobs are harder than football."

Randle grew up dirt-poor in the cotton fields of east Texas. For most of his childhood he was supported by a single mother who earned $23 a week as a maid. The family of four lived in a wood shack with a corrugated tin roof, an outhouse, and a bathtub that consisted of a bucket and a sponge. It was a hard life.

Certainly, there are guards and centers throughout the league who wring their hands and wish Randle had been raised as a spoiled rich kid because those humble roots have turned him into a monster on the football field.

"It makes me work," Randle says. "I want to give my family as much as I can. If it takes me working seven days a week to do it, I'll do it."

Randle's teammates call him "Motor," and he's usually revving pretty high. He used to tape sofa cushions to trees as a youngster, but he has replaced them with heavy bags like those used by boxers. He has been known to rope a log to his waist and run up

and down hills with it. "I had to tell the neighbors he wasn't crazy," his wife, Rosie, says.

"Going against him [in practice] is harder than going against anyone in the game," says guard Randall McDaniel, Randle's long-time teammate. "He doesn't know how to take breaks. You know he's coming full go, no matter if he's hurt, sick, whatever. He's coming a hundred percent every time."

Without that drive, it is unlikely Randle would have made it to the NFL. His older brother Ervin starred at Baylor before launching an eight-year career as an NFL linebacker. But John's SAT scores forced him to play at Trinity Valley Community College in Athens, Texas. He later transferred to Texas A&I, where he earned Little All-America honors as a senior, but that still placed him far from the spotlight. He was an undersized interior lineman (Randle is 6 feet 1 inch, 282 pounds now, but he weighed much less at the time) from a small school, and he went unclaimed in the 1990 draft.

As Randle remembers, "It was then that I told God, 'If you just give me one chance, I'll never look back and say, "What if?"'"

Randle got his chance, and he was starting for Minnesota by his second season. He was voted to his first Pro Bowl in 1993, but he soon found key teammates (such as Pro Bowl defensive tackle Henry Thomas) and coaches (such as defensive coordinator Tony Dungy) moving on. So Randle picked up any slack that had existed in his routine.

He got into even better shape and refined his

"He doesn't know how to take breaks. You know he's coming full go, no matter if he's hurt, sick, whatever. He's coming a hundred percent every time."
— Randall McDaniel

already-nifty moves. He also became an amateur detective, looking into his opponents' backgrounds to tailor his distracting on-field chatter. Enemy quarterbacks constantly tell their blockers not to listen to Randle, but by the fourth quarter the mile-a-minute talker usually has them distracted and frustrated.

As if he needed the extra advantage. Since 1991, Randle has more sacks (84½) than any other player in the NFL. In 1997, he led the league with 15½. That accomplishment goes from impressive to unbelievable when you consider that he plays in the middle, where he rarely gets an open route to the quarterback.

"John is the toughest player I play," Green Bay's Brett Favre says. "On artificial turf he's unblockable."

Noting Randle's exemplary effort and high-octane performance, the Vikings made him (briefly) the most highly paid defensive player in the history of the NFL in February, 1998.

"There is only one John Randle," club vice president Jeff Diamond says, explaining the hefty investment. "If there is a player worthy of this type of contract, it is John. He is the heart and soul of our defense."

Randle's rags-to-riches story was complete.

#93 JOHN RANDLE, Defensive Tackle

YEAR	TEAM	TACKLES	SACKS	FUM REC	INT	YDS	AVG	TD
1990	Minnesota	21	1.0	0	0	0	—	0
1991	Minnesota	58	9.5	0	0	0	—	0
1992	Minnesota	56	11.5	1	0	0	—	0
1993	Minnesota	59	12.5	0	0	0	—	0
1994	Minnesota	47	13.5	2	0	0	—	0
1995	Minnesota	47	10.5	0	0	0	—	0
1996	Minnesota	58	11.5	0	0	0	—	0
1997	Minnesota	71	15.5	2	0	0	—	0
CAREER TOTALS		417	85.5	5	0	0	—	0

Jerry Rice

San Francisco 49ers

When Jerry Rice was in junior high school in tiny Crawford, Mississippi, he decided to cut school one day. The principal saw him and gave chase. Impressed with the boy's speed, the administrator (after catching him and spanking him thoroughly) directed him to the football coach.

That principal, his name forgotten, has been cursed by a generation of NFL defensive backs. Without his meddling, they figure, maybe Rice would have become, say, an electrician.

Football fans used to argue about whether Rice was the best wide receiver of his day. Then he started setting records—most touchdowns in a season (22 in 1987…in only 12 games!), most touchdowns in a Super Bowl (3, twice), most career catches in the postseason (120). Then folks started debating who was the greatest receiver of all time, Rice or Don Hutson. And Rice set more records— most career receptions, receiving yardage, and touchdowns, most receiving yards in a season (1,848 in 1995), etc., etc. Now, the only question is whether Rice is the greatest NFL player ever, at any position.

Few who have played with or against him would vote otherwise.

Wymon Henderson wouldn't— not after a particular reception Rice made against him in 1993.

"I never even saw the catch,"

Henderson, then a Rams' cornerback, said afterward. "I had one of his arms. I had him pinned. I didn't think it was possible for him to catch the ball. When I saw him still running, I thought, 'How in the world did he catch the pass?'"

It's a question that has been asked often. Rice is 6 feet 2 inches, 200 pounds, relatively average by NFL standards. He is not a Jordanesque leaper, and his speed is surpassed by many other receivers—during time trials, anyway. As former 49ers safety Ronnie Lott once said, "Jerry has four-six speed on Tuesday and four-two

"I think he believes that if they covered him with eleven guys," Young says, "he should still be open and win the game."

speed on Sunday. Nobody outruns him in a game."

That's the thing: On Sundays, no one is better than Rice.

"He's the talent you look for to define all the skills," says R.C. Owens, the former 49ers receiver who is an executive assistant with the club. "He runs the field, pattern-wise, with great precision. He

gets off the line. He has three speeds, and changes them at any time. He has great hands. He can react to the ball wherever it is."

What sets Rice apart from other pass-catchers—and apart from the cornerbacks who are trying to stay with him—is devotion to his craft. He used to get equipment manager Ted Walsh, a left-hander, to warm him up for lefty quarterback Steve Young's passes. The fluid patterns Rice runs, the ones that look so effortless, are the product of countless, tedious hours spent working on routes before and after regular practice.

"I think he believes that if they covered him with eleven guys," Young says, "he should still be open and win the game."

Rice's running form was perfected by numerous sessions with a personal trainer, who helped him limit the bounce in his stride. His footwork was refined by jumping rope. And his physical stamina—which might compare favorably to a distance runner's—is equally manufactured. As soon as each season ends, Rice starts on his conditioning. His daily wind-sprint regimen usually starts with "accelerators": gain speed for 20 yards, sprint at full throttle for 60, decelerate for 20, then turn around and immediately do it 13 more times.

"I think it would blow people away to know how hard Jerry works during the week," retired tight end Brent Jones says. "And I'm talking about people on other teams, not the fans. Jerry runs hard—every play, every day."

He ran hard while setting 18 NCAA Division II records at Mississippi Valley State, and he ran hard when the 49ers traded up to take him in the first round in 1985. Since then, Rice has spanned the gaps of 49ers greatness. Among others, he has caught passes from Joe Montana and Steve Young, taken orders from Bill Walsh and George Seifert, run plays called by Mike Holmgren and Mike Shanahan.

Rice played 188 games over 12 seasons without missing one. Then the unthinkable happened. He suffered a major knee injury in the first game of 1997, made an amazing recovery to return for the next-to-last game, then hurt a different part of the knee.

Fans worried that the injuries might induce Rice to retire. The opposite is true.

"[I learned] just how much I loved this game," he says. "The fire's still inside. [This injury] was meant to happen, to make me realize what football means to me."

And what Jerry Rice means to us.

#80 JERRY RICE, Wide Receiver

YEAR	TEAM	NO	YDS	AVG	TD
1985	San Francisco	49	927	18.9	3
1986	San Francisco	86	1,570	18.3	15
1987	San Francisco	65	1,078	16.6	22
1988	San Francisco	64	1,306	20.4	9
1989	San Francisco	82	1,483	18.1	17
1990	San Francisco	100	1,502	15.0	13
1991	San Francisco	80	1,206	15.1	14
1992	San Francisco	84	1,201	14.3	10
1993	San Francisco	98	1,503	15.3	15
1994	San Francisco	112	1,499	13.4	13
1995	San Francisco	122	1,848	15.2	15
1996	San Francisco	108	1,254	11.6	8
1997	San Francisco	7	78	11.1	1
CAREER TOTALS		1,057	16,455	15.6	155

Barry Sanders

Detroit Lions

Talk to NFL players about Barry Sanders, and you begin to hear some interesting things.

"He's better than I was," one of them says.

"The things Barry does—whew!—I just wish I could do them," says another.

The first speaker is Walter Payton, the NFL's all-time leading rusher. The second is Emmitt Smith, a four-time rushing champion. Their responses are not uncommon. Some football players get respect from their peers; Barry Sanders attracts something more like awe.

"All you have to do is watch Barry run the ball once," Bills running back Thurman Thomas says. "That's all. Just see him carry the ball one time, and you'll understand that the man does things with that football that I don't think anyone else can do."

At 203 pounds, Sanders is no NFL giant. But as someone once said, he looks like a man who stood 6 feet 5 inches and weighed 240, then got hit on the head with a sledgehammer until he leveled out at 5-8. His thighs are as thick and as sturdy as the pillars of the U.S. Capitol, and they allow him to perpetrate moves that defy belief.

"Barry Sanders is the only guy who can go east and west at the same speed at the same time," Minnesota linebacker Dwayne Rudd says.

Or as former Detroit nose tackle Jerry Ball once observed, "By the time you get to where Barry is, he's not there anymore."

A favorite pastime of both teammates and opponents is recounting their favorite "Barry plays." Former Bills linebacker Darryl Talley selects one

from a 1991 game against the Lions. Talley and Cornelius Bennett hit Sanders at the same time, and the running back actually spun on his hands and his helmet—his knees never touching the ground—before escaping.

"That's still the craziest thing I've ever seen," Talley says. "I had him. Biscuit [Bennett] had him. And he spins on his helmet . . . that made no sense. It got so bad out there that we were laugh-

ing at each other because he was making us miss so bad."

That's Sanders, the proverbial genie in a bottle. When he played the Vikings during his rookie season, they demanded to see his jersey after the game; he had eluded so many arm tackles, they were sure he had coated the shirt with Vaseline.

And keep in mind that Sanders has done it all without a stellar cast around him. The Lions have

won only one playoff game during his tenure in Detroit. He has had a few standout blockers, such as tackle Lomas Brown and center Kevin Glover, but never a great line. He rarely has played with a fullback, and for several years the Lions did not employ a tight end.

Some superstars might have complained about the conditions. With Sanders, that's a ludicrous proposition. This is a humble, deeply religious man who consistently shuns the spotlight. He had to be talked into attending the Heisman Trophy presentation ceremony in 1988 (he won the award after setting 13 NCAA season records at Oklahoma State), and he turned down an invitation to President George Bush's inaugural dinner because he had to study. Sanders never trash talks, never loses his tem-

per. He gets water for his offensive linemen during time outs. His end zone celebration consists of locating the nearest official and calmly handing him the ball. When he signed his first contract with the Lions in 1989, he tithed 10 percent of his $2.1 million signing bonus to the Paradise Baptist Church in his hometown of Wichita, Kansas.

"Barry is a great player," says Glover, who recently went from Detroit to Seattle, "and Barry is a great man. He's the kind of person you brag about knowing."

And he keeps on running and running. Since his dazzling rookie year, the men to whom he has most often been compared—in particular, Smith and Thomas—have been slowed by the wear and tear of the position. Meanwhile, Sanders seems to get better every year. In 1997 he was held to a total of 53 yards in his first two games, then went on a 14-game rampage and finished with 2,053 yards, the second-best total in league history. He topped 100 yards in each of those 14 games, an NFL record.

Now the only man with more career yards is Payton, with 16,726. Sanders goes into the 1998 season with 13,778, and no one doubts his chances of leaving on top (projections have him passing Payton in 1999).

"I'm not the biggest or fastest or quickest back in the game," Sanders says, "but I'm one of the more fortunate."

He's got it wrong, of course. We're the fortunate ones because we get to watch him run on Sundays.

#20 BARRY SANDERS, Running Back

YEAR	TEAM	RUSHING				RECEIVING			
		NO	YDS	AVG	TD	NO	YDS	AVG	TD
1989	Detroit	280	1,470	5.3	14	24	282	11.8	0
1990	Detroit	255	1,304	5.1	13	36	480	13.3	3
1991	Detroit	342	1,548	4.5	16	41	307	7.5	1
1992	Detroit	312	1,352	4.3	9	29	225	7.8	1
1993	Detroit	243	1,115	4.6	3	36	205	5.7	0
1994	Detroit	331	1,883	5.7	7	44	283	6.4	1
1995	Detroit	314	1,500	4.8	11	48	398	8.3	1
1996	Detroit	307	1,553	5.1	11	24	147	6.1	0
1997	Detroit	335	2,053	6.1	11	33	305	9.2	3
CAREER TOTALS		2,719	13,778	5.1	95	315	2,632	8.4	10

Deion Sanders

Dallas Cowboys

In his NFL debut with Atlanta in 1989, Deion Sanders returned his first punt 68 yards for a touchdown. Five days earlier he had blasted a home run for the New York Yankees. Just like that, Sanders became the only athlete to score an NFL touchdown and hit a major league home run in the same week.

Welcome to Prime Time.

In the ensuing years, a nation of sports fans would come to believe there was nothing Sanders could not do, no envelope he couldn't stretch. In January, 1995, he became the first man ever to play in both a World Series (he hit .533 for the Braves in 1992) and a Super Bowl (he intercepted a pass for the 49ers in game XXIX; a year later, he would catch a 47-yard pass for the Cowboys in game XXX). In 1996, he became the first NFL player in 36 years to start on both offense and defense in the same season. In 1997, he recorded his fourteenth touchdown return. For those keeping score, that's 7 interceptions, 3 punt returns, 3 kickoff returns, and 1 fumble recovery, all ending in pay-dirt. Of course, that doesn't count his 3 touchdown catches or the time he scored on a reverse against Philadelphia in the 1995 playoffs.

But Sanders's unique versatility sometimes obscures the fact that he does one particular thing—cover-

ing wide receivers—as well as anyone else who ever has played the game. "Deion is the first player to be able to dominate and dictate a game from the defensive back position," commentator John Madden says.

"He takes one-third to one-half of the field away from the offense," veteran receiver Willie (Flipper) Anderson explains. "He'll be playing man-for-man on one guy, and the rest of the secondary will be playing zone. The quarterback is afraid to throw at Deion, and that frees the safety to cheat over to the opposite side."

What makes Sanders so formidable? His surprising upper-body strength (he's rather slender at 6 feet 1 inch, 195 pounds) helps him jam receivers at the line. He can stop and

> "He studies and he studies. He knows his opponent inside-out long before he steps out on to the field to play."
> — Tom Holmoe

start on a dime, and he has the strong hands of a baseball player. But above all is that supernatural speed.

"If you throw the ball out there and your receiver has a step, it shouldn't matter how quick he is," says long-time NFL quarterback Wade Wilson. "Well, it matters in Deion's case. He would lay low, and when the receiver went by him, he made up the ground while the ball was still in the air. I've never seen anybody who has been able to do that. It's phenomenal, but he

can actually catch up to the ball. He's that fast."

Sanders is a natural athlete. He once played a baseball game for Florida State, went over to the campus track and ran a leg of the 4x100-meter relay (in his baseball pants), then jogged back to the diamond and slapped the game-winning hit in the Seminoles' second game. Last year, after finishing second in the National League with 56 stolen bases for the Reds, he reported to the Cowboys'

camp on August 27. He took part in two days of meetings and one noncontact practice, and started the season opener on August 31.

But don't be fooled. Sanders is also one of the hardest-working athletes you'll ever see. He rides his bicycle 5 to 12 miles most offseason mornings, and often plays basketball after practice. And he breaks down film like a scientist.

"Deion knows a tremendous amount about football," says Tom Holmoe, his former position coach in San Francisco. "He studies and he studies. He knows his opponent inside-out long before he steps out on to the field to play."

The image of the devoted student is far from Sanders's public picture. He wears $5,000 teal suits and more gold than an Egyptian pharaoh. He cut an album called *Prime Time*, with a single, "Must Be the Money," that hit the Top 10 on the R&B charts. He is not hesitant to boast of his abilities, or of his bank account. But teammates insist there is more to the man than meets the eye.

"These are things ya'll don't know about Deion because it doesn't get publicized," Cowboys guard Nate Newton says. "He doesn't drink. He doesn't do drugs. He doesn't cuss. He's a strong family man. He's only flashy when he's out in the public entertaining."

And he's never flashier, never more entertaining, than when he's running stride-for-stride with the NFL's best receivers, hoping a quarterback will buck the odds and throw the ball his way.

#21 DEION SANDERS, Cornerback

YEAR	TEAM	TACKLES	SACKS	FUM REC	INT	YDS	AVG	TD
1989	Atlanta	39	0.0	0	5	52	10.4	0
1990	Atlanta	50	0.0	0	3	153	51.0	2
1991	Atlanta	49	1.0	0	6	119	19.8	1
1992	Atlanta	66	0.0	1	3	105	35.0	0
1993	Atlanta	34	0.0	0	7	91	13.0	0
1994	San Francisco	37	0.0	0	6	303	50.5	3
1995	Dallas	28	0.0	0	2	34	17.0	0
1996	Dallas	45	0.0	3	2	3	1.5	0
1997	Dallas	29	0.0	0	2	81	40.5	1
CAREER TOTALS		377	1.0	4	36	941	26.1	7

Junior Seau

San Diego Chargers

When Junior Seau was a senior at Oceanside High School in southern California, he met then-Chargers quarterback Dan Fouts at a local function. Fouts knew that Seau was a two-position star, and he asked the young athlete whether he would be playing tight end or linebacker at USC.

"I'm not sure," Seau replied.

"Play linebacker," Fouts advised. "They make more money."

It was a wise audible by the quarterback. Twelve years later, Seau signed a six-year, $27.1 million contract extension with the Chargers that made him, at the time, the highest-paid linebacker in the history of the sport.

Seau was thrilled about the cash, to be sure, but the deal meant more to him. "This is more of a contract to make sure I'm home and performing in front of the people who watched me grow," he said at a press conference.

Seau is the essence of a hometown hero, an affably bombastic football star who owns a highly visible hip-hop clothing line (Say Ow! Gear) and San Diego's most popular sports establishment (Seau's, The Restaurant). But part of the reason he is so popular in California's southern extreme is not because of what he has, but because of what he has given to get there.

Tiaina Seau, Jr., split his early life between Oceanside, a working-class community with strong military ties, and American Samoa, his ethnic homeland. He didn't speak English until he was 7. He lived in a poor neighborhood, in a house

so full of relatives he slept between the washing machine and the mop in the family garage.

But it was clear early on that Seau's physical gifts were vast. After achieving All-America status at USC, Seau went to the Chargers in the first round of the 1990 draft, making him the first selection of the Bobby Beathard era in San Diego.

Soon he was the most popular player on the team.

It's hard not to be won over by someone who plies his trade with such intensity. Seau plays every game, every snap, as if his life depends on it. Teammates call him the Tasmanian Devil. His trademark "Lightning Bolt" dance makes him the target of opposing fans' outrage, but it's a crowd pleaser at Qualcomm Stadium.

"With Junior, it's spontaneous," says Bobby Ross, his former head coach. "He makes a lot of money, but he'd probably play for free. I know it's true because he practices pretty much the same way."

Seau constantly pushes himself to improve. He spends about 10 hours a week in the weight room during the offseason, further chiseling one of sport's most unbelievable bodies. He can bench press nearly 500 pounds and curl 170-pound dumbbells. And yet he can run the 40-yard dash in 4.61 seconds.

"If I had a hundred-thousand dollars," former Chargers defensive end Burt Grossman once said, "I'd train Junior and have him lose twenty pounds, then put him in the decathlon. I'd put him up against Dan [O'Brien] and Dave [Johnson]—together. There's nothing he can't do athletically."

Such a work ethic has allowed Seau to improve nearly every season since 1990. He always made big plays, always set himself apart as one of the best athletes on the field. But in the early days he also was prone to overzealous mistakes. Since then, his mental game has caught up to the physical, and that is why you now hear him mentioned in the same sentence as all-time greats such as Dick Butkus and Jack Lambert.

Seau has been to the last seven Pro Bowls. He has been the Chargers' leading tackler in 64 of the 125 games he has started. (He has missed only two NFL starts despite a litany of injuries, including a pinched nerve in 1994 that caused him to lose all strength in his left arm for entire quarters of play.)

"Junior Seau is the best defensive player we've faced, I'd say—and by a pretty good margin," Bill Belichick said when he coached the Cleveland Browns. "He does it all. He can play at the point of attack, he chases down plays, he plays the run, he plays the pass. He's a guy nobody's really been able to stop."

And Seau is equally unstoppable when it comes to civic activity. In 1991, he channeled his charitable efforts into the Seau Foundation, a nonprofit body that raises money for drug awareness, child abuse prevention, and college scholarships. His work won him the NFL Man of the Year award in 1994.

#55 JUNIOR SEAU, Linebacker

YEAR	TEAM	TACKLES	SACKS	FUM REC	INT	YDS	AVG	TD
1990	San Diego	85	1.0	0	0	0	—	0
1991	San Diego	129	7.0	0	0	0	—	0
1992	San Diego	102	4.5	1	2	51	25.5	0
1993	San Diego	129	0.0	1	2	58	29.0	0
1994	San Diego	155	5.5	3	0	0	—	0
1995	San Diego	129	2.0	3	2	5	2.5	0
1996	San Diego	138	7.0	3	2	18	9.0	0
1997	San Diego	97	7.0	2	2	33	16.5	0
CAREER TOTALS		964	34.0	13	10	165	16.5	0

Shannon Sharpe

Denver Broncos

Shannon Sharpe on gaining respect: "You're only great if you win something. I mean, Alexander wasn't Alexander the Mediocre or Alexander the Average. He was Alexander the Great, and there's a reason for it."

Shannon Sharpe on his high school education: "I didn't graduate cum laude. I graduated 'Thank you, Lawdy.' With my grades, I couldn't have gotten into prison."

Shannon Sharpe on the prospect of seeing single coverage against the Packers in Super Bowl XXXII (to a *Denver Post* columnist): "If they cover me one-on-one and beat my butt, then I will renounce my citizenship, move out of the country, and leave all my assets in a bank account in your name."

Meet the NFL's human quote machine. Sportswriters, worn down by a generation of tight-lipped "no comments," love Sharpe, the six-time Pro Bowl tight end. Turn on your tape recorder, ask a simple question, and wait for the click that signals the end of the tape. "Ever since Shannon was a little boy, there was never a dull moment," says his sister, Libby Sharpe. "Unless he was asleep."

Opponents, of course, are not always so amused. Shannon apologized to New England in 1996 after an HBO camera caught him pick-

ing up a sideline phone during a 34-8 Denver win and blurting, in mock alarm: "Mr. President, we need the National Guard, because we are killing the Patriots!"

Sharpe's act would be preposterous if he weren't able to back up his words with sensational deeds. His uncommon speed and soft hands have established him as one of the best tight ends of all time—which isn't bad for someone who spent much of his early career known as Sterling Sharpe's Little Brother.

Sterling, now a studio analyst for ESPN, was one of the most prolific wide receivers of his era. He broke the NFL single-season reception record with 108 catches in 1992, then upped the ante with 112 in 1993. But his career, once on a path to the Pro Football Hall of Fame, ended when he dislodged two vertebrae in his neck late in the 1994 season. It was a stunning blow to

"Ever since Shannon was a little boy, there was never a dull moment," says his sister, Libby Sharpe. "Unless he was asleep."

both Sharpes, who always have been best friends.

The two were born in Chicago, but when their neighborhood started getting too rough, their mother sent them to live with their grandparents on a farm outside of Glennville, Georgia (population: 5,000). Their nearest neighbor was a half-mile away. That meant plenty of sibling competition, and plenty of defeats for Shannon, who was three years younger.

For years, it seemed that Shannon never would emerge from his brother's shadow. Sterling received a full scholarship to South Carolina, was a

first-round draft choice of the Green Bay Packers in 1988, and burst onto the scene with a total of 145 catches in his first three NFL seasons. Shannon wound up at Division II Savannah State. He went in the seventh round (the 192nd overall pick) in the NFL draft as a wide receiver to the Broncos in 1990, and caught a total of 29 passes in his first two years. He was one game away from being cut as a rookie, but responded with an inspired performance in the Broncos' final preseason game.

Then-head coach Dan Reeves is credited with encouraging Shannon and converting him to tight end. Once at the bigger position, he began a gradual ascension to stardom.

What held Sharpe back in the first place? It may have been that sports was just too easy for him. He averaged 30 points and 15 rebounds as a high school basketball player, and won the Georgia state championship with a triple jump of 49 feet 5 inches. It wasn't until he decided to devote himself completely to football that he blossomed.

Sharpe started haunting the Broncos' weight room, and it wasn't long before he was sporting 21-inch biceps, a 52-inch chest, and a body-fat count of 4 percent. "It's tough to match up with Shannon," Broncos quarterback John Elway says. "There aren't many guys who can bump Shannon because he's too strong for them."

And there are fewer, especially among linebackers and strong safeties, who can run with him stride for stride. Sharpe led all NFL tight ends with 72 catches for 1,107 yards in 1997, and is atop the pack with 383 receptions since 1993.

"He's one of the five best players in the league," New York Jets head coach Bill Parcells says.

#84 SHANNON SHARPE, Tight End

YEAR	TEAM	NO	YDS	AVG	TD
1990	Denver	7	99	14.1	1
1991	Denver	22	322	14.6	1
1992	Denver	53	640	12.1	2
1993	Denver	81	995	12.3	9
1994	Denver	87	1,010	11.6	4
1995	Denver	63	756	12.0	4
1996	Denver	80	1,062	13.3	10
1997	Denver	72	1,107	15.4	3
CAREER TOTALS		465	5,991	12.9	34

Bruce Smith

Buffalo Bills

When quarterback Jeff George has nightmares, there's a good chance they'll involve a game he played while with the Colts in 1990. It seemed as though every time George dropped back to pass that day, Buffalo's Bruce Smith was in his face. By the end of the game, Smith had dropped George 4 times.

If George can take any solace in such a pounding, it's in the fact that he has plenty of company. Fifty-five NFL quarterbacks, from Steve Grogan to Jeff Blake, have found themselves buried beneath Smith since 1985. Surely, more victims await number 78.

Smith is the perfect pass-rushing machine. At 6 feet 4 inches, 273 pounds, with hardly an ounce of fat, he moves like a hungry velociraptor.

"He has an unbelievably explosive first step," says Patriots tackle Bruce Armstrong, a long-time rival and admirer. "He's relentless, and once you get into him you must stay on him because he has such great closing speed. He can get to the quarterback even when you think the ball should be gone."

A native of Norfolk, Virginia, Smith put the Virginia Tech football program on the map. He won the Outland Trophy as the nation's best collegiate lineman in 1984 and the Bills made him the first pick in the 1985 draft. He started immediately, and by 1987 he was earning the first of 10 Pro Bowl bids. (Among NFL defensive ends, only Reggie White has more.)

Smith has been consistently excellent throughout

his career, but his 1990 season stands out. It was then he terrorized NFL passers for a career-high 19 sacks and 4 forced fumbles. He helped Buffalo make it to Super Bowl XXV, where he staked the team to a 12-3 lead by tackling Giants quarterback Jeff Hostetler for a safety. (The Bills eventually lost 20-19.)

During the 1990 season, Smith declared himself Lawrence Taylor's successor as the best defensive player in the league.

> "I demand attention. I feel that the only way I'll get better is if I have at least two people on me. It makes me rise to the occasion."

That did not sit well in some circles, but those close to Smith know he wasn't boasting. He simply was pointing out what the average fan might not see: the double- and triple-team blocks he constantly faces.

"I consider it an insult if it doesn't happen," Smith says about the tag-teaming. "I demand attention. I feel that the only way I'll get better is if I have at least two people on me. It makes me rise to the occasion."

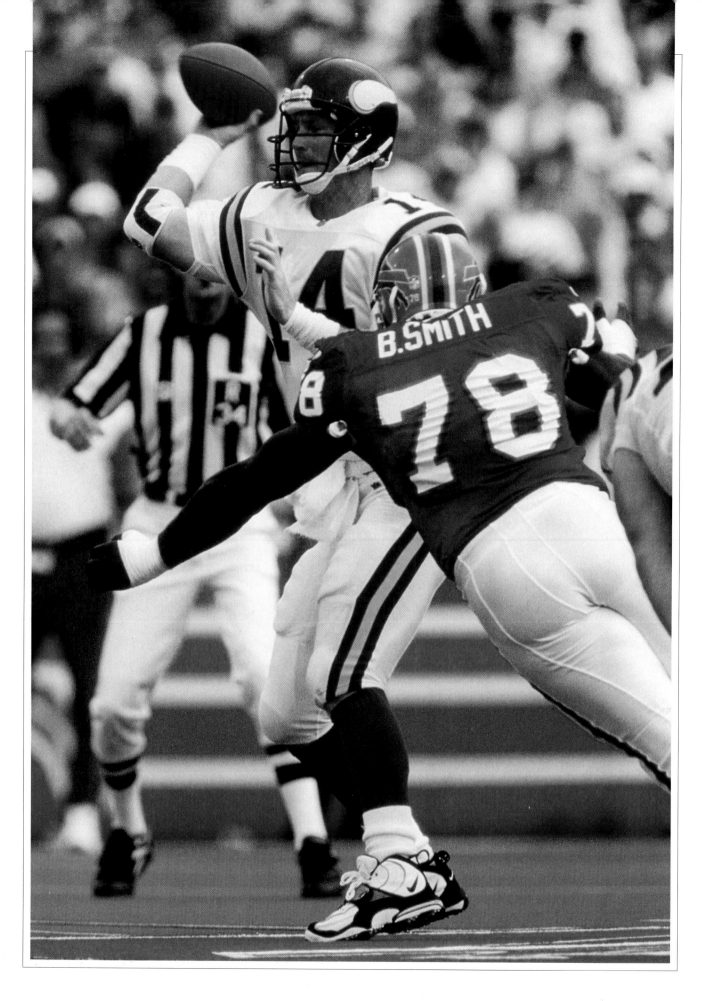

Anyway, Smith's claim was hard to contradict. Some said he was purely a speed rusher; they never had to play against him. "Most people think that because he's so quick he has only an outside pass rush," says veteran quarterback Warren Moon (sacked 6 times, tied for sixth on the Smith List). "But he's so powerful he can bulldoze over you."

A more common complaint claimed Smith was weak against the ground game. That may have been true early in his career, but his run defense has improved greatly over the years. He has recorded four seasons with 100-plus tackles, the most ever among Bills defensive linemen.

And as the millennium approaches, Smith is busy proving one more thing: endurance. "He knows he's good, and it's fun to do something you're good at," says Marv Levy, who retired as Bills head coach after the 1997 season. "He must have a great thirst for the game to be playing with this much vigor for this long."

In 1997, his thirteenth NFL season, Smith overcame two sore knees and an aching shoulder to lead the AFC with 14 sacks, and once again was on his way to Honolulu. Only White (176½) has more career sacks than Smith's 154, and they share the all-time postseason record of 12. (Sacks have been an official NFL statistic since 1982.) Smith and White are the only defenders to record at least 10 sacks in 11 different seasons. Yet Smith still is able to leave the young guys shaking their heads.

As rookie defensive end Marcellus Wiley reported in 1997, "People were telling me, 'Wait until you see Bruce do some things. You think we're good players? Wait until you see Bruce.' He amazed me from the first snap."

#78 BRUCE SMITH, Defensive End

YEAR	TEAM	TACKLES	SACKS	FUM REC	INT	YDS	AVG	TD
1985	Buffalo	48	6.5	4	0	0	—	0
1986	Buffalo	63	15.0	0	0	0	—	0
1987	Buffalo	78	12.0	2	0	0	—	0
1988	Buffalo	56	11.0	0	0	0	—	0
1989	Buffalo	88	13.0	0	0	0	—	0
1990	Buffalo	101	19.0	0	0	0	—	0
1991	Buffalo	18	1.5	0	0	0	—	0
1992	Buffalo	89	14.0	0	0	0	—	0
1993	Buffalo	108	14.0	1	1	0	0.0	0
1994	Buffalo	92	10.0	2	1	0	0.0	0
1995	Buffalo	107	10.5	1	0	0	—	0
1996	Buffalo	120	13.5	1	0	0	—	0
1997	Buffalo	87	14.0	0	0	0	—	0
CAREER TOTALS		1,055	154.0	11	2	0	0.0	0

Emmitt Smith

Dallas Cowboys

Only three times has a running back won both an NFL rushing title and a Super Bowl championship in the same season. The three players who did it were Emmitt Smith, Emmitt Smith, and Emmitt Smith.

Before Smith rolled deuces in 1992, 1993, and 1995, some considered it an unattainable feat. Relying so heavily on a single person, they claimed, makes a team too one-dimensional. But Smith's versatility and durability, not to mention a roster of talented teammates, made him unique.

"When you have to go with a running back who is the complete back—receiving, blocking, and running—I feel Emmitt is the guy," says Franco Harris, a Hall of Fame runner for the Pittsburgh Steelers in their championship seasons.

Smith's impact on the Cowboys has been immense. When he held out to start the 1993 season, the team dropped its first two games, to Washington and Buffalo. Smith saw Dallas head coach Jimmy Johnson looking weary and anxious on television, and he decided it was time to return. No team ever had overcome an 0-2 start to win the Super Bowl, but with Smith leading the way—he would win his third rushing title—the Cowboys went 12-2 over the remainder of the regular season and waltzed through the postseason.

Playing Buffalo in Super Bowl XXVIII at the end of the year, the Cowboys found themselves trailing 13-6 at halftime. So they put the ball in Smith's hands and watched him sink the Bills with 91 second-half yards. He finished with 132 yards and 2 touchdowns, and was named most valuable player of the game.

"Emmitt was making so many pretty moves, he was about to shake me out of my drawers," Dallas guard Nate Newton said afterward.

Smith has a full assortment of shakes and bakes, but he isn't a magician along the lines of Barry Sanders. And that's Emmitt in a nutshell: not the very best at any one category, but good at everything. He isn't a bulldozer at 209 pounds, but he is shockingly powerful for his size. Ask former 49ers linebacker Bill Romanowski, whom Smith flattened to set up the go-ahead touchdown in the 1992 NFC Championship Game.

Smith's speed could be described as adequate. As

Whitey Jordan, his offensive coordinator at Florida, said, "He may not go eighty yards on one play, but he can go forty yards twice."

Really, Smith's skills are harder to pinpoint. "What separates him from other backs is explosiveness," Dallas quarterback Troy Aikman says. "Once he gets the ball, he has tremendous vision. He's hard to bring down because he's so strong in his hips and his legs."

Smith's most important body part, though, is his oversized heart. That vital organ was never more in evidence than on January 2, 1994. Visiting the Giants in the last week of the season, with the NFC East title and home-field playoff advantage on the line, Smith suffered a first-degree separation of his right shoulder in the first half. The pain was excruciating. His teammates had to help him up after every carry. But Smith would not relent. He handled

> "Emmitt was making so many pretty moves, he was about to shake me out of my drawers."
> — Nate Newton

the ball 17 times after the injury and led Dallas to a 16-13 overtime victory, gaining 41 of the Cowboys' 52 yards on the winning drive.

But it is hard to remember this gritty, win-at-all-costs competitor when Smith is standing in a school auditorium. Kids love the guy. His modest height (5 feet 9 inches) and elfin grin make him look more like a mascot than a football player. But as Smith hit the circuit of schools in the Dallas-Fort Worth area, something began to bug him. Here he was telling students to stay in school, and he didn't have a college diploma—he had left Florida 13 units shy of his degree. So Smith fulfilled a promise to his mother and went back to school, earning a bachelor's degree in public recreation in May, 1996.

Smith has had a lifetime full of honors. He gained 8,804 yards (third best ever among preps)

at Escambia High School in Pensacola, Florida; he set 58 school records in three years at the University of Florida; he is one of only four NFL players to win three consecutive rushing titles; he set an NFL record with 25 touchdowns in 1995; he owns league postseason marks for career 100-yard games (7) and touchdowns (20); he was portrayed, along with the legendary Red Grange, on the cover of a book that celebrated the league's seventy-fifth anniversary; he has three Super Bowl rings.

But the diploma was special. Above all, it was a measure of resilience, which is what Emmitt Smith is all about.

#22 EMMITT SMITH, Running Back

YEAR	TEAM	RUSHING				RECEIVING			
		NO	YDS	AVG	TD	NO	YDS	AVG	TD
1990	Dallas	241	937	3.9	11	24	228	9.5	0
1991	Dallas	365	1,563	4.3	12	49	258	5.3	1
1992	Dallas	373	1,713	4.6	18	59	335	5.7	1
1993	Dallas	283	1,486	5.3	9	57	414	7.3	1
1994	Dallas	368	1,484	4.0	21	50	341	6.8	1
1995	Dallas	377	1,773	4.7	25	62	375	6.1	0
1996	Dallas	327	1,204	3.7	12	47	249	5.3	3
1997	Dallas	261	1,074	4.1	4	40	234	5.9	0
CAREER TOTALS		2,595	11,234	4.3	112	388	2,434	6.3	7

Kordell Stewart

When Bill Tobin visited the University of Colorado as the Indianapolis Colts' director of football operations, he was especially keen on scouting the wide receivers. Three of them—Charles Johnson, Michael Westbrook, and Rae Carruth—wound up as eventual first-round choices in the NFL draft. But somebody else caught Tobin's eye.

"The quarterback would outrun the wide receivers," he said.

That quarterback was Kordell Stewart, and he was something to watch at Colorado. He left with records of 456 completions and 7,770 yards of total offense, earning second-team *Associated Press* All-America honors as a senior. Still, he was on the board until the sixtieth pick of the 1995 NFL draft. "We made a mistake, I'll say that," Bears coach Dave Wannstedt later said, no doubt speaking for most of the league's other coaches.

It was the Steelers who landed Stewart, and head coach Bill Cowher soon took to calling him "Slash." It was in reference to a punctuation mark, as in "Kordell Stewart: quarterback/wide receiver/running back."

Stewart was a throwback to the days of the Single-Wing. He could throw, he could run, he could catch. He even punted as a rookie. And

though he was determined to play quarterback full-time, he didn't mind the varied experience. "Playing wide receiver gave me an opportunity to be out there and actually see the defenses," he says. "That's better than being on the sideline holding a clipboard."

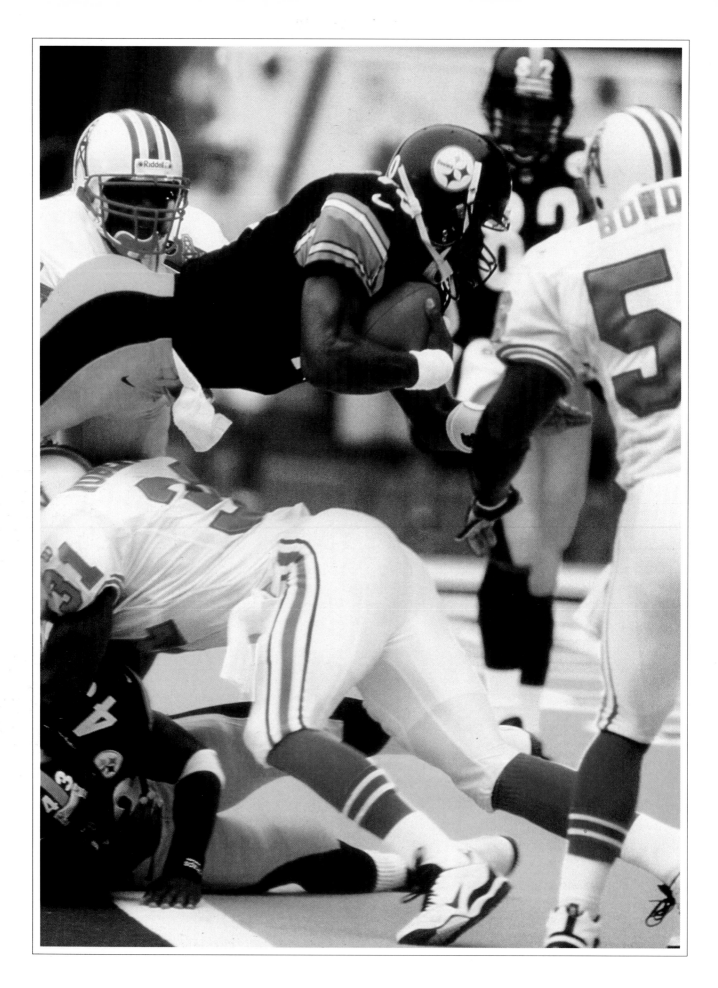

Stewart's versatility, combined with an infectious smile and an unmasked love for the game, made him one of the most popular NFL newcomers of the decade. Pittsburgh fans loved it when he entered the game to run the option in short-yardage situations. They went nuts when he set the NFL record for longest scoring run by a quarterback (80 yards against Carolina in 1996).

But a problem arose as Stewart gained experience: He was too good to employ as a novelty. The Steelers needed him on the field for every offensive play, so they made him their starting quarterback in 1997. "Slash" was gone, but the full-time quarterback left in his place was far more valuable.

"Every time he gets on the field, the possibilities are unlimited," Pittsburgh center Dermontti Dawson says. "If it's a broken pass and the receivers are covered downfield, he can make something happen. And he gives you a lot of options—a *lot* of options."

Indeed, Stewart's mobility makes a tangled mess of opposing defensive schemes. "Mobility threatens a defense, keeps it more honest," former NFL head coach Sam Wyche says. "And it's a fail-safe in case a play doesn't work. Kordell Stewart may add even more importance to this trait because he's basically a running back playing quarterback."

"You have to account for that guy," Cowher says. "When you have a guy who can run, you'd better not get out of your rush lane, you'd better worry about containing, you'd better not be running in coverage with your back turned because this guy can take off."

And you'd better not stack the line and dare him to throw because it is increasingly obvious that he can burn you with passes, too. In 1997, Stewart became the first Steelers quarterback to surpass 3,000 yards (3,020) and 20 touchdowns (21) in a season since Terry Bradshaw.

Twenty-one touchdown passes might not seem like a bombing run in comparison to Brett Favre and

Drew Bledsoe, but when you add Stewart's 11 rushing touchdowns you get a sense of his impact. Only six NFL teams scored more points than Pittsburgh last season, and only four won more games.

"You can evaluate the quarterback position any way you want," Cowher says. "But I've always believed the bottom line is taking your football team and putting it in position to win games. He's done that very well, and he's getting better at it each week."

Stewart still needs to reduce his interception total (he threw 17 in 1997) and gain consistency. But remember, he has had only one season as a starter. He already has infused his teammates with confidence.

"I'd like to have Kordell's future," Steelers running back Jerome Bettis says.

A lot of people would settle for Stewart's present.

#10 KORDELL STEWART, Quarterback

YEAR	TEAM	ATT	COMP	PCT	YDS	TD	INT	RATING
1995	Pittsburgh	7	5	71.4	60	1	0	136.9
1996	Pittsburgh	30	11	36.7	100	0	2	18.8
1997	Pittsburgh	440	236	53.6	3,020	21	17	75.2
CAREER TOTALS		477	252	52.8	3,180	22	19	72.7

Dana Stubblefield

Washington Redskins

Like a fumble bouncing erratically on the turf, Dana Stubblefield's life could have gone a couple of different directions. Stubblefield lost all the men to whom he was closest—his father, his uncle, his grandfather. But new people always managed to enter the gaps just when he needed them most.

Stubblefield was a 6-year-old living in Cincinnati when his father walked out on him, his mother Thelma, and three siblings. The family lived in English Woods, which sounds lovely but really was one of the city's poorest neighborhoods. Dana's size didn't prevent his schoolmates from picking on him relentlessly. His Uncle Jimmy toughened him up, taught him to fight, but Jimmy died in a car accident when Dana was 14.

When Stubblefield was in eighth grade, the family moved to Cleves, Ohio, a small town about 20 miles down the Ohio River. And when his mom moved back to Cincinnati, he stayed with his grandparents. Then his grandfather, whom Stubblefield credits with teaching him the value of hard work, died.

This time the shy teenager moved onto a 216-acre farm owned by family friends, Terry and Martha Heath. There was plenty of work to be done on the land. He baled hay, cleaned stalls, and fed the horses.

And by the time he left for the University of Kansas, he was considered family.

And the Heaths weren't the last influences to lay a hand on Stubblefield's shoulder. When he got homesick and struggled at Kansas, assistant coach Mitch Browning, the man who had

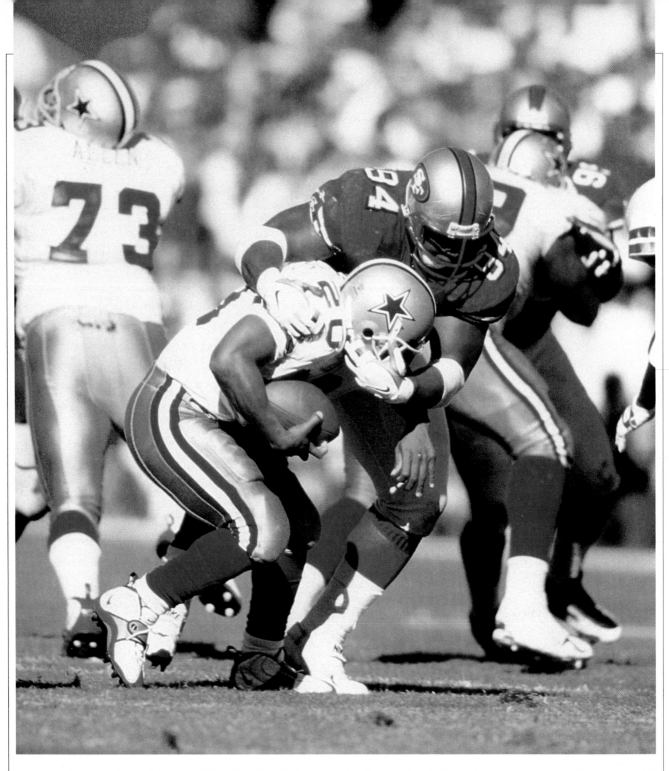

recruited him, kept his head level. All of these benefactors were taken by Stubblefield's quick smile and gentleness. And it was with their help that he became a first-round draft choice of the San Francisco 49ers in 1993.

At that point he could pretty much take care of himself, as Steelers running back Barry Foster found out in Stubblefield's first pro game. "I guess he was coming full speed," Stubblefield recalled. "And I just stopped him. He hurt me. It numbed both my shoulders. But I knew right there I could play in this league."

Stubblefield started as a rookie and led the 49ers with 10½ sacks. He led the team again with 8½ in 1994, and afterward made the first of two consecutive Pro Bowl appearances. "Dana's one of the big premier players," 49ers linebacker Lee Woodall says. "He puts a lot of fear in a lot of different offenses."

Then came Stubblefield's disappointing 1996

season, when he finished with only 1 sack and sometimes seemed lost in the action. Before his twenty-seventh birthday, some were calling him a has-been.

That set the stage for 1997, when the mighty run-stuffer became the heart of the NFL's top-ranked defense. Stubblefield had a career-best 15 sacks and was named *Associated Press* NFL defensive player of the year. In a memorable Monday night game against Philadelphia, with three defensive teammates on the bench, he sacked

> "He has a certain fire inside of him," San Francisco linebacker Ken Norton says. "All you have to do is rub him a little to get it out."

Ty Detmer and Bobby Hoying 4 times to trigger a 24-12 victory. Hey, they should have known not to rile him with all that talk about being washed up. "He has a certain fire inside of him," San Francisco linebacker Ken Norton says. "All you have to do is rub him a little to get it out."

A certain fire? Stubblefield once lost two front teeth and chipped another in a violent collision—during pregame warmups. In any case, his season-long assault made him one of 1998's most coveted free agents, and it was Washington that won the bidding. The Redskins' first order of business probably was tailoring a pair of football pants to fit their new star.

Stubblefield has legs that look as if they belong in Jurassic Park. He has to buy size-50 pants, then have them taken in to fit his comparatively trim 42-inch waist. He maintains his leg strength by squatting 700 pounds. "Some scouts were concerned that he didn't have a big upper body," says Fred Roll, the strength coach at Kansas. "His upper body *is* big, but his legs are so big it makes his upper body look small."

Yet the 6-foot 2-inch, 302-pound Stubblefield isn't exactly rooted to the ground. On one play in 1994, he leaped over Atlanta running back Erric Pegram with perfect hurdler's form, and continued in stride to sack Jeff George, causing a fumble.

It all sounds pretty frightening, but Stubblefield's old friends aren't intimidated. "He's like a big teddy bear," Martha Heath says, blowing the defensive tackle's cover.

#94 DANA STUBBLEFIELD, Defensive Tackle

YEAR	TEAM	TACKLES	SACKS	FUM REC	INT	YDS	AVG	TD
1993	San Francisco	64	10.5	0	0	0	—	0
1994	San Francisco	39	8.5	0	0	0	—	0
1995	San Francisco	40	4.5	0	1	12	12.0	0
1996	San Francisco	39	1.0	1	1	15	15.0	0
1997	San Francisco	65	15.0	0	0	0	—	0
CAREER TOTALS		247	39.5	1	2	27	13.5	0

Derrick Thomas

Kansas City Chiefs

Derrick Thomas is a Chief, but he also is a falcon. Make that *the* falcon.

Kansas City defensive coordinator Gunther Cunningham, unhappy with his unit's performance in 1996, rewrote some 500 pages of the Chiefs' playbook for 1997. The new base defense was called the Falcon, and it revolved around a position of the same name. The man who fills that position is Thomas, who resembles nothing more than a swift bird of prey when zeroing in on NFL quarterbacks.

"You have to know where he is at every moment on the football field," Broncos head coach Mike Shanahan says. "There are few players you can say that about."

The whole point of the Falcon is to make Thomas hard to locate. He may line up as the right defensive end in a three-point stance. He may be a stand-up linebacker on the left side. He may even drop into pass coverage.

Unfortunately, Thomas did not get to take full advantage of his new opportunities. He missed six starts while recovering from a torn triceps in 1997. Still, that didn't stop him from recording 9½ sacks (tied for sixth in the AFC) and making the Pro Bowl for the ninth time in his nine-year career. If he is voted to the game again in 1998, he'll tie Lawrence Taylor and Mike

Singletary for the most visits by a linebacker.

Thomas was the first player selected under head coach Marty Schottenheimer and general manager Carl Peterson, a regime that has taken the Chiefs to seven playoff appearances since 1989. And in that span he has collected sacks the way some people collect Beanie Babies. Thomas currently ranks

twelfth on the all-time list with 107½. He set the single-game record by sacking Seattle's Dave Krieg 7 times in 1990, a performance that helped him total 20 for the season. The speed of his assaults has resulted in 39 forced fumbles during his career. He also has recovered 16 fumbles.

Half of Thomas's work is accomplished with a lightning-fast first

"As great an athlete as he is, it is the stuff he does away from the game that stands out to me. That is what makes him a really big man."
— Chris Martin

step. "You have your fast outside linebackers who pass rush in a Nickel situation," retired tackle Anthony Muñoz said, "and then you've got Derrick Thomas, who is pretty much in a class by himself. I've never really played against a guy who had that initial quickness off the ball."

About the only place Thomas can be found as frequently as the

opponent's backfield is in the various branches of the Kansas City public library.

His signature social program is Third and Long, a literacy campaign that he promotes by spending each home Saturday of the football season in a library, reading to underprivileged kids. His work won him the 1993 NFL Man of the Year Award and the 1995 Byron White Humanitarian Award, the latter from the NFL Players Association.

"As great an athlete as he is, it is the stuff he does away from the game that stands out to me," former Chiefs linebacker Chris Martin says. "That is what makes him a really big man."

Thomas received another honor when he was asked to present the keynote address at the Memorial Day observance in 1993 at the Vietnam War Memorial. His father, Robert Thomas, was an Air Force captain whose B-52 bomber was shot down over Vietnam in December, 1972, when Derrick was 5 years old. The mission for which Robert Thomas gave his life, strangely enough, was called Operation Linebacker Two.

Other than a father, Derrick had everything a child needs to get by, but that didn't prevent him from making a lot of bad decisions in his junior high and early high school years. He lived near the projects in Miami, close enough to find trouble without looking for it.

"I had one-thousand-dollar bikes sitting at my house," Thomas says, "but I wanted to go out with my friends and steal a bike that was probably worth less than fifty dollars."

That came to an end when a judge sentenced him to a stint in the Dade Marine Institute, a state-run alternative school for troubled teens. There were no frills at DMI, and his time there showed him a path he did not want to travel.

"When I got back to high school, I had to make a decision on what I was going to do," Thomas says. "Was I going to be a positive member or a negative member of society? Positive growth won out."

Years later, Thomas's positive growth continues to result in negative yardage for the quarterbacks of the NFL.

#58 DERRICK THOMAS, Linebacker

YEAR	TEAM	TACKLES	SACKS	FUM REC	INT	YDS	AVG	TD
1989	Kansas City	75	10.0	1	0	0	—	0
1990	Kansas City	63	20.0	2	0	0	—	0
1991	Kansas City	79	13.5	4	0	0	—	0
1992	Kansas City	67	14.5	3	0	0	—	0
1993	Kansas City	43	8.0	1	0	0	—	0
1994	Kansas City	86	11.0	3	0	0	—	0
1995	Kansas City	71	8.0	1	0	0	—	0
1996	Kansas City	58	13.0	1	0	0	—	0
1997	Kansas City	55	9.5	0	0	0	—	0
CAREER TOTALS		597	107.5	16	0	0	—	0

Reggie White

The 1993 NFL offseason was the first in the era of unrestricted free agency, and as the dollars began to fly around, the Eagles' Reggie White soon emerged as the grand prize. White was a stunning mix of brawn, size (6 feet 5 inches, 290 pounds), and agility—and nearly everyone wanted him.

Philadelphia fans staged a desperate "Rally for Reggie" to keep him in town. Browns owner Art Modell forbade any swearing in the club offices for the two days White was in town. In the end, though, the lineman chose Green Bay. Why? God told him to go there.

You can construct your own ideas about divine communication, but there is no doubting the depth of White's beliefs.

"In this day and age, when you're not sure who's genuine and who isn't," Packers head coach Mike Holmgren says, "I can tell you he's the real thing."

White has deep religious roots. The only time he got into trouble in high school was when he tried to read the Bible in his sociology class. He was licensed as a minister of the gospel at age 17. By the time he was winning All-America honors at the University of Tennessee, writers had dubbed him the Minister of Defense. White tells dazed quarterbacks, "God loves you," when he helps them up after a sack.

Many athletes fill in their work schedule with charitable activity, but White's involvement goes way beyond handshakes and three-day camps for kids. One of his latest projects, Urban Hope, is a sweeping program that seeks to provide start-up grants and loans to prospective small business owners in inner-city areas across the country.

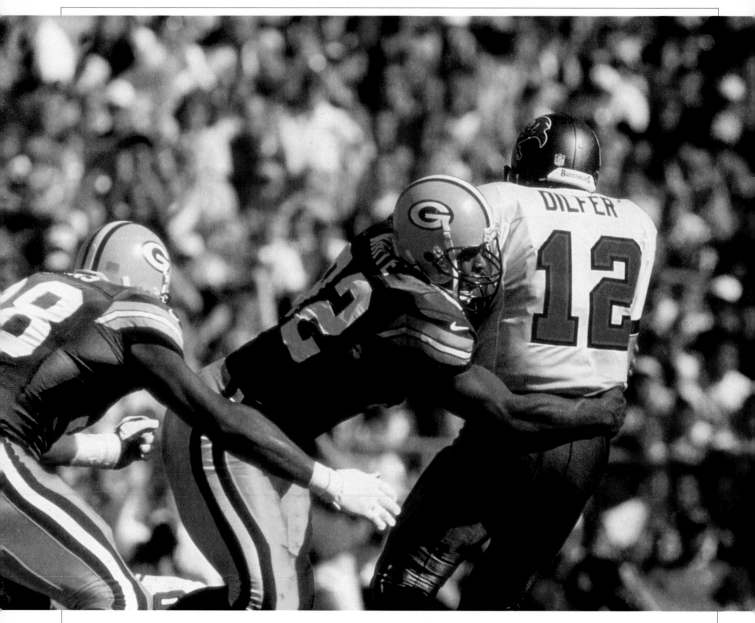

And he's a pretty good football player, too.

Actually, when you get right down to it, White might be the best defensive end ever to assume a three-point stance. He stuffs the run like Gino Marchetti and rushes the passer like Deacon Jones, the two ends who joined him on the NFL's 75th Anniversary Team.

"He's a guy you definitely want on your side rather than against you," Green Bay quarterback Brett Favre says. He should know. A year before they became teammates, White slightly separated Favre's shoulder on a sack.

White played a 20-game USFL season with the Memphis Showboats before becoming an NFL rookie. In his first game with the Eagles in 1985, he had 2½ sacks and deflected a pass that a teammate intercepted and returned for a touchdown. It was a fitting introduction.

White didn't make the Pro Bowl that season, but he made it every year thereafter—12 successive seasons, the NFL's longest streak since the 1970 merger. He is the league's all-time sack leader with 176½. He set a Super Bowl record with 3 against the Patriots in XXXI, and he fell 1 short of the reg-ular-season record with 21 in 1987—in only 12 games. At the same time, opponents continually run to the opposite side of the field.

"Find me the guy who says Reggie White has lost a step," Dallas tackle Erik Williams said in 1993. "Get him down on the field and I'll make him line up against Reggie so he can see for himself."

White's impact on the Packers was both immediate and obvious that season.

"We went from twenty-three on defense to two," Holmgren says, referring to Green Bay's NFL statistical ranking pre- and post-Reggie, "with no noticeable dramatic personnel changes, except for one man."

And it wasn't simply because of the big man's physical skills. He is the consummate team leader, a gravel-voiced giant who works hard every minute and never backs down from an opinion.

"He's probably the most unselfish team player I've ever been around, and it rubs off. If you were to look at one guy whose demeanor and whose mode of living is an example for all of us to follow, it's Reggie White."
— Fritz Shurmur

"He's probably the most unselfish team player I've ever been around, and it rubs off," Packers defensive coordinator Fritz Shurmur says. "If you were to look at one guy whose demeanor and whose mode of living is an example for all of us to follow, it's Reggie White."

White has entered a love affair with Green Bay, a wind-chilled, predominately white city that couldn't be more unlike his hometown of Chattanooga, Tennessee. When his Inner City Church of Knoxville, Tennessee, was torched by arsonists in January, 1996, the people of Wisconsin gave him more than $300,000 in donations. White cried when he publicly thanked the contributors. And when it was announced that the region might need another area code, one of the leading contenders was 920—a nod to the new favorite son and his jersey number.

That's why the entire state went into mourning when the Packers announced White's retirement in April—and why the cheese tasted extra sweet when he suddenly unretired a few days later.

#92 REGGIE WHITE, Defensive End

YEAR	TEAM	TACKLES	SACKS	FUM REC	INT	YDS	AVG	TD
1985	Philadelphia	100	13.0	2	0	0	—	0
1986	Philadelphia	98	18.0	0	0	0	—	0
1987	Philadelphia	76	21.0	1	0	0	—	0
1988	Philadelphia	133	18.0	2	0	0	—	0
1989	Philadelphia	123	11.0	1	0	0	—	0
1990	Philadelphia	83	14.0	1	1	33	33.0	0
1991	Philadelphia	100	15.0	3	1	0	0.0	0
1992	Philadelphia	81	14.0	1	0	0	—	0
1993	Green Bay	98	13.0	2	0	0	—	0
1994	Green Bay	59	8.0	1	0	0	—	0
1995	Green Bay	46	12.0	0	0	0	—	0
1996	Green Bay	36	8.5	3	1	46	46.0	0
1997	Green Bay	45	11.0	2	0	0	—	0
CAREER TOTALS		1,078	176.5	19	3	79	26.3	0

Aeneas Williams

Arizona Cardinals

At a family Christmas gathering a few years ago, Aeneas Williams's aunt played an audiotape she had found lying around. Aeneas had made the recording on his Mr. Microphone toy as a child, but had forgotten about it. On the tape was a boy's innocent voice declaring, "I'm going to be a pro football player someday, and I'm going to be the best defensive back in the NFL."

It was quite a boast. Then again, it was quite a young man who made it. Thanks to a stable family—especially his disciplinarian father, a lab supervisor for Union Carbide—Williams emerged from one of New Orleans's toughest school systems to earn his place as a Pro Bowl cornerback and a solid citizen.

"My father always told us, 'If you have to choose between me and the police, you'd better choose the police,'" Williams says.

In the long run, Williams chose God, football, and community service. One of four teammates at Fortier High School who eventually would play defensive back in the NFL—the others were Ashley Ambrose, Maurice Hurst, and Kevin Lewis—he was offered an academic scholarship to Dartmouth. But Williams turned down the Ivy League, opting to follow his brother Achilles to Southern University. (Aeneas and Achilles, you may know, were characters glorified by the Greek poet Homer in *The Iliad*. As Aeneas Williams says, "We had the Trojan War in our backyard every weekend.")

Aeneas did not attend Southern to play sports. He took accounting classes and got involved in student government for two years before he decided to try football. By his senior year (when he played as a graduate student, having already earned his degree) he tied for the NCAA Division

I-AA lead with 11 interceptions.

Williams started for the Cardinals as a 1991 rookie and never looked back. He has been a starter in the last four Pro Bowls. He led the NFC in interceptions in 1994 and tied for the lead in 1991. And he has done it while playing for a team that has compiled a record of 38-74, without a single winning season, since his arrival.

"He might be the best I've been around," says Buddy Ryan, his head coach in 1994–95. "He can do it all. He can tackle. He can cover. He can run. He takes a challenge."

No one challenged him more than Ryan, whose attacking 46 defense forced its cornerbacks into steady man-for-man coverage. And remember, at 5 feet 10 inches Williams gives up size to the likes of Dallas's Michael Irvin (6-2) and Washington's Michael Westbrook (6-3). Williams hasn't backed down yet.

"With Aeneas you know it's going to be good, clean, hard-nosed football," says another friendly rival, Philadelphia's Irving Fryar. "It's always a joy to be able to go out and compete against a guy like that."

Opposing quarterbacks might not find the experience as joyful. More and more of them are being victimized by what Williams calls the "quick six." Six times he has returned interceptions for touchdowns—only 3 away from Ken Houston's all-time record.

Williams actually called Houston a few years ago to pick his brain about techniques and strategy. But that is nothing new. Williams, an avid student of the game, has sought out veterans such as Gill Byrd, Ronnie Lott, and Everson Walls to compare notes.

Williams works hard on his conditioning, too. He keeps himself in such good shape that he was the only Cardinals player to post a sub-2-minute time when the team opened its 1994 training camp with a mandatory 880-yard run. "I hate mediocrity," he says. "I disdain 'average' with a passion. If I feel there's an area where I'm average, then I'm

> "I hate mediocrity. I disdain 'average' with a passion. If I feel there's an area where I'm average, then I'm going to go to the woodshed and find out how I can raise my level."

going to go to the woodshed and find out how I can raise my level."

When it comes to his personal life, Williams shouldn't spend any time in that woodshed. He gets up at 5 A.M. every day to pray and read the Bible, and he hosts a weekly Bible study for teammates and their wives. He also doesn't drink, and he doesn't swear.

"I've told young players who come in here," Arizona defensive backs coach Larry Marmie says, "'If you're going to pick somebody to follow, watch this guy. Watch him in the meetings, watch him on the practice field, and watch him in the game.'"

Above all, watch him on the quick-out pattern, or he's liable to burn you for a quick six.

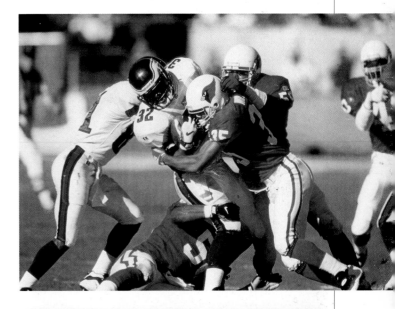

#35 AENEAS WILLIAMS, Cornerback

YEAR	TEAM	TACKLES	SACKS	FUM REC	INT	YDS	AVG	TD
1991	Phoenix	48	0.0	1	6	60	10.0	0
1992	Phoenix	48	0.0	1	3	25	8.3	0
1993	Phoenix	42	0.0	2	2	87	43.5	1
1994	Arizona	46	0.0	1	9	89	9.9	0
1995	Arizona	58	0.0	3	6	86	14.3	2
1996	Arizona	74	1.0	1	6	89	14.8	1
1997	Arizona	70	0.0	0	6	95	15.8	2
CAREER TOTALS		386	1.0	9	38	531	14.0	6

Steve Young

Steve Young was riding high when he left Brigham Young University in 1984. Not only had he set an NCAA record by completing 71.3 percent of his passes as a senior, he was a great-great-great-grandson of Brigham Young, Mormon patriarch and the man for whom the school is named. Talk about a campus hero!

But Young shunned the NFL and signed instead with the Los Angeles Express of the United States Football League. It wasn't what you'd call a great career move. The USFL foundered financially and couldn't consistently attract large crowds. For a developing young quarterback, it must have seemed that things couldn't get worse.

They did.

The Tampa Bay Buccaneers made Young the first pick in the 1984 supplemental draft, and the left-handed passer soon found himself running for his life behind a rickety offensive line. He went 4-15 as a starter during two seasons with Tampa Bay, throwing 11 touchdown passes against 21 interceptions. Again, things couldn't get any worse.

Again, they did.

Most players would have relished a trade to the powerful 49ers in 1987, but for a quarterback it meant sitting on the bench while Joe Montana performed his miracles. In his first four seasons in San Francisco, Young started only 10 games. He grew increasingly impatient. By the end of the 1990 season, he was 29 years old and wondering when he'd be an NFL starter.

It happened the next season as Montana recuperated from elbow surgery. It would prove to be a painful time for both men.

No matter what Young did in his first three seasons by the Bay—and he led the NFL in passer rating all three years—the fans (not to mention some of his teammates) would not accept him. They moaned about Young not getting the ball to Jerry Rice enough, about his frequent downfield runs, and his inability to win the big games.

A less stable individual would have caved in under the pressure. But Young is a fun-loving prankster who used to tell his Express center, Mike

Ruether, "Snap the ball over my head, and let's see what happens."

Young continued to speak with his actions, and he turned the corner in 1994, when he bolstered his individual excellence with a victory in Super Bowl XXIX. He even set a Super Bowl record with 6 touchdown passes in the 49ers' 49-26 win over San Diego. Finally, this was his team.

The funny part is, Young has no regrets about his early hurdles. "The Buccaneers were worthwhile," he says. "The Express was worthwhile. Now I feel like all those trials and struggles kind of make sitting on top of the mountain a nicer place to be."

The view from that mountaintop must be something else. In a purely statistical index, Young is the greatest quarterback in NFL history. It isn't even close. After leading the league with a rating of 104.7 in 1997, he joined Sammy Baugh as the only men ever to win 6 NFL passing titles. In the 78-year history of the league, only 22 times has a quarterback exceeded a rating of 100 in a season; 5 of them belong to Young. Montana, with three 100+ seasons, is the only other passer with more than one. And of the two, Young actually has the better winning percentage in San Francisco, .726 to .719.

Brigham Young's descendant has emerged as an unflappable leader and an accurate passer.

"He can throw the three levels of ball—the three-step, eight-to-fifteen yards, and the line of scrimmage to infinity—with ability," says Milt Davis, an NFL scout for 30 years. "Not too many can do all three well."

Not many have Young's mobility, either. Some have called him a running back with an arm. Among quarterbacks, only Randall Cunningham ever ran for more yardage than Young's 3,728, and only Jack Kemp scored more touchdowns than Young's 37.

Yet he is the same down-to-earth guy whom teammate Harris Barton once jokingly accused of tossing each new trophy and game ball he

> "The Buccaneers were worthwhile. The Express was worthwhile. Now I feel like all those trials and struggles kind of make sitting on top of the mountain a nicer place to be."

earned into the back seat of his car. Young takes constant ribbing because of his taste for inexpensive clothes and used automobiles. Don't be fooled, though. He also is a sharp-witted student who earned his law degree from BYU in 1994. He claimed he took the classes to keep from getting bored in the offseason.

"The thing that keeps me young is the constant quest for perfection," he says.

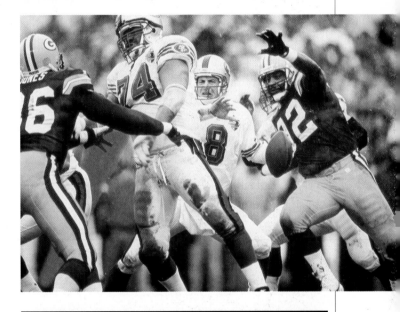

#8 STEVE YOUNG, Quarterback								
YEAR	TEAM	ATT	COMP	PCT	YDS	TD	INT	RATING
1985	Tampa Bay	138	72	52.2	935	3	8	56.9
1986	Tampa Bay	363	195	53.7	2,282	8	13	65.5
1987	San Francisco	69	37	53.6	570	10	0	120.8
1988	San Francisco	101	54	53.5	680	3	3	72.2
1989	San Francisco	92	64	69.6	1,001	8	3	120.8
1990	San Francisco	62	38	61.3	427	2	0	92.6
1991	San Francisco	279	180	64.5	2,517	17	8	101.8
1992	San Francisco	402	268	66.7	3,465	25	7	107.0
1993	San Francisco	462	314	68.0	4,023	29	16	101.5
1994	San Francisco	461	324	70.3	3,969	35	10	112.8
1995	San Francisco	447	299	66.9	3,200	20	11	92.3
1996	San Francisco	316	214	67.7	2,410	14	6	97.2
1997	San Francisco	356	241	67.7	3,029	19	6	104.7
CAREER TOTALS		3,548	2,300	64.8	28,508	193	91	97.0

10 Players to Watch

PETER BOULWARE
LB, Baltimore Ravens
Boulware made an immediate impact. His 11 1/2 sacks in 1997 were just 1 shy of the NFL rookie record.

WARRICK DUNN
RB, Tampa Bay Buccaneers
Dunn made the Pro Bowl after rushing for 978 yards and catching a team-high 39 passes in 1997.

TERRY GLENN
WR, New England Patriots
His hamstring injury healed, Glenn is hoping to match the NFL-rookie-record 90 receptions he made in 1996.

KEYSHAWN JOHNSON
WR, New York Jets
Johnson is confident enough to demand the football, and he was good enough to catch it 70 times in 1997.

RYAN LEAF
QB, San Diego Chargers
At 6 feet 5 inches, 240 pounds, Leaf might be strong enough to carry the Chargers as a rookie.

PEYTON MANNING
QB, Indianapolis Colts
The son of former NFL passer Archie Manning, Peyton might be the best-prepared rookie quarterback ever.

JAKE PLUMMER
QB, Arizona Cardinals
In his first NFL possession, Plummer drove the Cardinals 98 yards for a late touchdown against Philadelphia.

DARRELL RUSSELL
DT, Oakland Raiders
Enormous (6-5, 310 pounds) and agile, Russell is back at his true position after a season at defensive end.

ANTOWAIN SMITH
RB, Buffalo Bills
Smith was impressive enough to dislodge Thurman Thomas as the team's rushing leader in 1997.

ZACH THOMAS
LB, Miami Dolphins
Thomas started at middle linebacker and was Miami's leading tackler in his second season.

PHOTO CREDITS

Bill Amatucci 17, 48, 51, 85, 132

Greg Banner 158

James V. Biever 20, 62

Peter Brouillet 11, 22, 42, 55, 57, 70, 118, 133

Jimmy Cribb 95

Greg Crisp 75, 78, 135, 136, 146

Tom Croke 82

Scott Cunningham 13

David Drapkin 59, 94, 111, 113, 120, 140

Mike Eliason 37, 100

Tracy Frankel 90

Gerald Gallegos 66

E.B. Graphics 143

George Gojkovich 73, 112

Seth Harrison 29

Thearon Henderson 81, 138

Glenn James 6, 53, 65, 69

Paul Jasienski 25, 31, 150

Diane Johnson 158

Allen Kee 35, 86, 98, 101, 106, 114, 124, 153, 159

Al Kooistra 128

L.C. Lambrecht 16, 84

Michael Martin 45, 142

Al Messerschmidt 67, 93, 151, 159

Darrell McAllister 36, 64

Tom Miller 14, 50

Mike Moore 99

Marty Morrow 23

Steven Murphy 21, 33, 38, 109

Patrick Murphy-Racey 137

Vincent Muzik 77

Bernie Nuñez 87, 127

Al Pereira 125

Richard Pilling 130

Evan Pinkus 9

Joe Poellot 39, 46, 47, 121

Louis Raynor 145

Mitchell B. Reibel 43, 52, 126, 131

Joe Robbins 40, 88

Bob Rosato 24, 27, 32, 54, 74, 80, 89, 110, 152

Todd Rosenberg 7, 148

Joe Sandaus 41

James D. Smith 8, 30

Paul Spinelli/NFLP 18, 72, 103, 104, 119, 134, 156, 158, 159

Brian Spurlock 158

Robert Skeoch 105, 107, 108

Allen Dean Steele 10

David Stock 12

David Stluka 19, 44, 58, 60, 61, 96, 117, 144, 147, 157, 159

Kevin Terrell/NFLP 63

Greg Trott 26, 28, 56, 115, 116, 112, 123

Tony Tomsic 97, 158

Jim Turner 34, 83, 129, 158

Ron Vesely 15, 49, 76, 79, 92

Tony Williams 91

Bill Wood 139

Thad Woodward 149

Michael Zagaris 1, 68, 71, 102, 141, 154, 155